The REDI Network

Redi-Network.com

Presents:

The Royal Penthouse Suite

Foreword by Rene McCoy

I met Christopher Dallas spontaneously for a quick drink to see if the connection we had over the dating app and phone really had some real weight to it. Our "date" lasted for hours over multiple drinks, great conversation, shared experiences and what felt like a million laughs in between. It was clear that we found one another attractive however, as the evening would come to a close, we discovered through conversation that we were both looking for something quite different, in terms of relationship goals.

Over the course of the years, we have maintained a healthy, balanced and mutually respectful friendship. A friendship where we have unpacked numerous relationships, casual or otherwise.

Now let's talk about the Royal Penthouse Suite shall we?

This book is a history lesson, reality show, brotherly advice and therapy session all rolled into one. I appreciated Dallas's use of Hotel Room Types to drive home the fact that we need to understand that relationships have levels, complete with perks and reward points. One can easily misinterpret said levels if one is not truly and actively engaged in seeking the clues given, and *not* given. This book highlights the importance of how having a healthy EQ plays out in the ever changing ever complicated world of relationships.

After reading this book I felt myself wishing that things were simpler like in the 1950s, while also wanting all the empowerment that women have in today society minus some of the toxic social constructs. I enjoyed the small but truly relevant glimpses of the male mind at work (either with or without them having an erection). The lighthearted and satirical writing is indicative of Dallas's personality and caring spirit and is a compliment to his previous work.

As the reader you will undoubtedly identify with some of the people described in this book, whether directly or indirectly. My advice to you is to enjoy the read, take some notes, and have a drink handy, you might need it.

To:
My friend
Nichole
Thank you for your input!

Rest in Peace

Table of Contents

Chapter 1: Why Write this book? *8*

SECTION ONE: How We Got Here *12*

Chapter 2: Naked Breasts, Elbows & Hammers *12*

Chapter 3: Social Cash & The Handbook *25*

Chapter 4: 1950 .... *35*

Chapter 5: Mouth Wide Open *40*

Chapter 6: Erection versus Emotions *53*

SECTION TWO: Early and Online Dating *64*

Chapter 7: The Parking Garage *64*

Chapter 8: The Online Profile Dilemma *71*

Chapter 9: 12 Years to Save *80*

SECTION THREE: Casual Sex *93*

Chapter 10: Destination: Casual Sex *93*

Chapter 11: Your Hotel Suite Accommodations *103*

Chapter 12: Living Room PowerPoint Presentation *109*

Chapter 13: The Miseducation of Ms. Out of Town *119*

Chapter 14: Tear Up the Contract *129*

SECTION FOUR: Long Term Relationships *146*

Chapter 15: The Emotional Bank Account *146*

Chapter 16: You = Your Experiences *160*

Chapter 17: The Bridges that Connect us *168*

The Royal Penthouse Suite

Chapter 1:

Why Write this book?

I'm thinking. I'm thinking. Give me a second.

Ok what was your question again? What's a dating-type "situation" that I have not personally experienced? That's a good question.

Let me ask you, by "situation," do you mean like: "*Single and lonely?"* Absolutely I've been in that boat. How about: "*Overloaded, overwhelmed and dumbfounded with too many casual sex options*?" Yes. And that time frame was so surreal the whole time it was happening. Or: Have I been *completely head over heels in love*? You bet! Another Situation: Married in a small chapel? I sure was.

Have I participated within every angle of the cheating triangle? That would a triple yes. 1- I've cheated on a girlfriend; 2- Been cheated on *by* my girlfriend; 3- I've been the "side-guy" to a woman cheating in *her* relationship.

What else? I've been in that early dating stage when I really, *really* liked someone and she just plain didn't like me back. I've been placed unceremoniously into *"the friend zone"* which is torture because I still "get to be around" someone I deeply like, and I have to *pretend like I don't like them so much*.

Have I done any *online dating*? Tons - on all kinds of different sites & apps. From those sites, the dates ranged from beyond excellent to boring as hell, to a full-fledged stalker to everything in-between.

Let's see I've: Been catfished. Stood-up. I've hooked up. Picked up. I've dated women I met in bars, clubs, back-yard cookouts, corporate meetings, academic conferences. All of that.

I appreciate you asking. Because sometimes I've thought to myself: What the hell *was* all of that?

Why did the universe expose me to such a full spectrum of dating, sexual, and romantic situations?

Maybe we're about to find out. And since we're on the subject of "situations," I've had endless discussions with female and male friends about *their* unique encounters as well. I feel like I have lived through some of their experiences.

Truth is, we're all trying to navigate the rough sea waters of relationships. I can only see this from my heterosexual perspective, but I'm guessing that this is the same roller coaster all humans ride when we all seek companionship, regardless of who we pursue in sex or love.

Personally, I try to think about what's behind all these dating, sexual, and romance stories. Meaning, how does society condone *some of my* behavior, while judging other parts of it? There are so many double standards. Also, so many people that judge themselves for their actions, or lack of actions.

It all leads to confusion at the least. Heartbreak at the worst. So many people searching for love, or at least to make themselves "feel better about themselves."

Maybe, just maybe, my experiences *and* those of my friends, and all the resulting conversations, were meant to be shared and discussed.

This is book 3 of 4 in a series on emotional intelligence. It is a discussion point on precisely how we can be more self-aware of the societal pressures and internal struggles that surround us during our quests for love and affection.

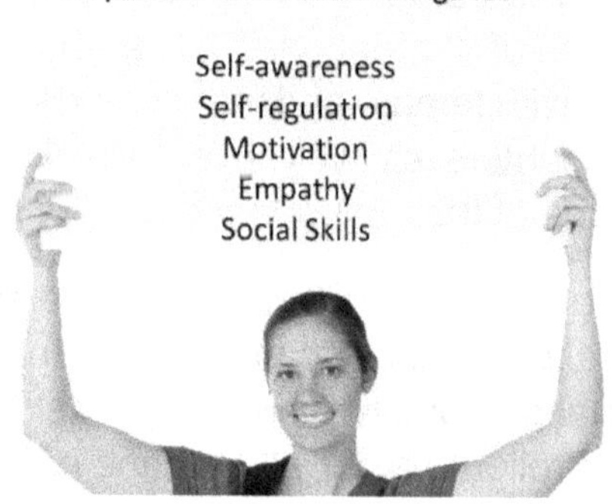

And these discussions aren't easy. There are so many harsh realities of egos, long-standing societal-constructs, and childhood traumas buried deep beneath our actions. We can share steamy-sex and funny-dating stories all day, but can we dig hard on how they impact us emotionally?

This book won't hold back on any of the details on raw sex and dating stories. It will gaze directly out of the author's eyes and observe the actions at the backyard cookout, the backseat of the car, and the heavy workload on the couch.

We'll dive into the deep waters of self-awareness and how it can save us precious time with relationships we don't need to pursue. Beyond that, we'll share how emotional intelligence (EQ) helps the entire dating community, even those we never meet. We'll be an accountant, sifting through the deposits and withdraws from our emotional bank accounts to balance our emotional relationship budgets.

Here's to those venturing into the early stages of dating someone brand new. Here's a toast to those currently at the hotel front desk, getting their room keys for the Suites of Casual Sex Relationships. Raise your glass for those in the established communities of long-term relationships who need more knowledge-of-self than any of us.

Cheers.

Section One: How We Got Here

CHAPTER 2: Naked Breasts, Elbows & Hammers

My buddy had been trying to tell me for years. But when I finally saw them, I was a bit upset with him.

They were magnificent. They were barely restrained by a sundress on a hot day in August. I vaguely remember overhearing some of the words spoken by the woman to whom they were attached.

I could check them out from a short distance away while sipping from my red cup. The more I *tried* to look away while at this backyard cookout, the more I looked over in their direction. I started imagining seeing them one day fully exposed in my living room.

That buddy of mine had indeed been trying to tell me for years that the woman living across the street from his sister had huge breasts and a teeny, tiny waist. He had told me that she was cute too and shapely from the waist down. So, when his sister threw one of her big, blowout, backyard summer events, I was there. And so were those breasts attached to the woman from across the street.

I turned to him:

That's who you were talking about? All this time man, you were talking about… her?

He reiterated that he had mentioned it many times before. And he was right, he had. But he didn't *convince* me that I should have taken action earlier. Since I couldn't go back in the past, it was time to act now.

"*Well dude, let's walk over there, introduce me.*" I was already scheming in my mind: A cute, small-waisted, big-breasted chick who keeps smiling at me from across the yard while she sips from her own red, plastic cup? Oh, she will fit quite nicely into my rotation – or maybe more. As we walked towards her, her breasts rose and fell with each breath she took. As she saw us coming her way, her smile intensified.

Where does all this come from? The coveting. The scheming. And how can discussions on emotional intelligence help? Let's take a quick trip to two different locations on planet earth to examine further and then we'll come back to this cookout.

The Battle over Breasts in Ocean City

Ocean City, Maryland. A regionally popular beach resort town. If you haven't been, it looks exactly like what you're picturing: A long beach. A busy boardwalk in summer, desolate during winter. A few seafood restaurants with patio seating. Small shops selling touristy beach items.

This tiny community plays a small but essential part in the evolution of gender dynamics and dating.

May 20, 2017. The Ocean City Beach Patrol got a memo on a new policy. The memo stated that the patrollers should only *document* complaints of women being topless. The memo instructed the patrols to *not* take any action. Specifically, it mentioned to not tell women that they must cover up.

Even if other beachgoers complain that the women should be covering up their breasts, just make a note and keep it moving. The memo said police officers will handle nudity complaints.

Social media went crazy, saying this is now a Topless Beach!

City Council got involved. They voted on the matter in June of that year with two different results.

- One: The council members placed a full ban on bare-chested women.
- Two: Five women sued that council. The paperwork for the lawsuit was filed that following January 2018.

During the court proceedings, the mayor of the resort town testified that he received calls and emails complaining about the women going topless. He placed a quote on social media:

> *"We have a responsibility to protect the rights of thousands of families who visit our beach and boardwalk each summer season."*

Fast forward to April 2020. Federal judge James Bredar showed he had a sense of what was coming. While he upheld the original City Council's right to ban topless women, he noted that the Supreme Court's treatment of sex and gender has evolved through the decades.

Judge Bredar's direct quote:

> *"This court questions whether the laws that distinguish between men and women based of (so called) public sensibilities can survive indefinitely".*

In other words, he sees a day where just because some people aren't ready to move past the concept of literally viewing women's breasts as sexual body parts, one day the courts *will* be ready.

Just not today.

Why not now? Because the people complaining on the beach still have the idea that us stupid men won't be able to control our fawning. Therefore, all of society is somehow at risk, even little kids. The idea exists that naked female breasts will bring out the 14-year-old kid in all adult males. And to an extent, that's true. For Today. It happened to an extent at that cookout, with me anticipating what those breasts might look like.

If you tell my friends and I that some beach has half-naked women on it, we just might be more apt to be there. ASAP! You mean we don't have to fly around the world to southern France or Brazil? Wow, it's time to celebrate! Thousands of guys have gone to Mardi Gras in New Orleans to catch a glimpse of women pulling out their breasts in exchange for beads.

But one day we'll get to a point where it's common place. One day, the novelty of seeing bare breasts will dissipate. Currently, as long as breasts remain taboo and sexualized then yes, it is indeed scandalous to have them exposed on a public beach.

Exposed Elbows & Knees in Qatar

Sexualizing *exposed female body parts* isn't limited to breasts at backyard cookouts or in beach towns in Maryland. In certain Muslim communities, the wearing of a jilbab covers the entire woman from head to toe. When a face veil (Niqab) and gloves are added, only the eyes are exposed to the outside world. The reasoning is strictly religious and is not an obligation. The Islamic subset of Salafism informs us:

"This is more suitable so that they will be known as pious women, and not be harassed. Practice of preventing women from being seen by men except by their closest male relatives. Men are not allowed to shake hands with women unless they are closely related to them."

The point is, parts of our global society aren't ready to trust men *not* to harass, stare, ogle women if certain body parts are visible.

So, let's return to that backyard cookout.

After an introduction, I was able to focus on keeping contact with her eyes: Keeping my vision away from the battle between her breasts and the sundress straining to contain them. Her continuous, flirtatious smile displayed a level of consent to my across-the-yard staring. And yes, we uh, "dated" on and off for few years following being introduced at that cookout. It all worked out.

But what if she *wasn't* ok with it? What happens when staring leads to unwanted advances during an otherwise family-oriented picnic?

Well, for one, a jilbab would prevent men like me from even knowing she had huge breasts. And since she wasn't my family, I wouldn't be allowed to speak to her. But that still doesn't give *her* the option.

We (*and just because it's a different culture, doesn't mean it's not still happening on our planet during our lifetimes, so it's "we"*) cover women from head to toe not just to keep stupid males from staring, but because we believe women aren't capable of "managing" those same males.

And not just that men will go crazy over seeing a sexualized body part, but that we'll be *justified* in doing so. So, that if we see a shoulder or an elbow or *gasp* a knee: We're ok to start potentially *harassing* that woman who dares expose herself. Sundresses at cookouts are included.

Bare female breasts in Ocean City. Elbows and knees in Qatar? There is no difference. If someone proposed that women be allowed to show their shoulders, elbows, or knees in parts of Qatar or Afghanistan, the wording of the pushback would

---

This is immoral. This is against family values. This crushes the very foundation of our society. Cover your children's eyes because women displaying their shoulders, elbows and knees will scar them for life!

---

read like the outcry in Ocean City:
No one in Ocean City or anywhere in western society is sexualizing female shoulders, elbows, or knees. The idea is laughable. But in parts of Qatar, that exposure would to be taken very seriously!

The double standard of course is: Men, showing those exact same body parts, aren't an issue at either location. Why?

- Because women *can* control themselves?
- Because men are still the pursuers of sex in any given culture?
- Because we can't objectify male body parts?

There's a difference between *sexual attraction* derived from a body part and *objectification*.

An "in-shape" male with his shirt off, broad shoulders, large, defined pectorals and 6-pack abs can absolutely be viewed as *sexually attractive*. Hell, he can even show it off to the public without anyone being offended or calling the beach patrol to file a complaint.

He's not objectified in the same way an "in-shape" woman with large, defined breasts would be if *she* were half naked on the beach? He's admired, but not objectified. Some might even see him as motivation to get in shape themselves! He's a walking billboard advertisement for your local gym. Give that man some applause!

What is an object?

An object does something for me, like a hammer or a lawnmower. I get something out of using that hammer, it helps me accomplish a goal.

Subconsciously, I get something from society out of accomplishing the goal of getting a woman to expose her breasts in private to me.

Add to that: Staring at woman's breasts when it's not reciprocated by her, also reduces her breasts to objects.

Society can see value in that bare-chested man for things other than his sexual attractiveness. We infer and then value that he is dedicated towards health and fitness. We infer and then value that he is confident and virile. He is a benefit to our society.

The bare-breasted woman is just seen for what her breasts can do for men in a sexual way. From that, children and families must be shielded from seeing those naked breasts because those breasts are emitting sexual-thought, radioactive frequencies into everyone's mind.

And of course, sexually aroused men are a plague to family values and the very foundation of society.

Like the woman at the cookout, her body parts drew me because of what those parts *could do for me*. Her breasts became an object. And like a hammer or a lawnmower, they exist only for one reason. In this case: to arouse men like me.

Even if you make breasts legally naked on every beach in America today, it's not as though we will immediately see breasts as non-sexual, maybe in a few years. We still can be sternly realistic about where we are today. Meaning today: Don't start walking up to me on the beach with your breasts fully exposed just because I'm the guy who wrote about dating and objectification versus sexual attraction and gender balance. If you do that, I would *not* be able to concentrate on forming complete or cognitive sentences.

We aren't there yet! We'll *all* get there, just like *I'll* get there. We are all a work in progress. Our collective emotional intelligence will help. This book is a guide for the discussions that can lead us there.

Disclaimer:

Am I saying that the folks complaining about nudity in Maryland or the wearers of jilbab are *wrong* for their views and we all need to be butt-naked on the beach by the end of next week? Of course not.

I'm using those examples and the backyard cookout to create a snapshot of where we are right now across multiple cultures. Currently, some parts of Europe and South America are on vastly different points on the spectrum and there is absolutely nothing wrong with that.

However, what I *am* saying is that, just like Judge Bredar, we can sense that in the future, we may view this topic differently. And that the dynamics on how we see gender roles are changing as well. The landscape has changed already just in the last ten years with the #MeToo movement and other advancements in how men view women. I cringe at some of my own sentiments in the 2010 writing of *Too Simple To Believe*.

Currently, men frequently still have the direct visual connection of *seeing* a woman and *thinking* about sex. And still today, all those conversations I've had with people about dating leave me with the impression that women still greatly underestimate how much men are driven by sexual desires.

Dating will change. Gender interactions will change. And between now and that future? Between 1950 and Naked Breasts being *no big deal* in Ocean City? The landscape of our culture can be altered by a population that is increasingly emotionally intelligent (EQ).

Specifically using the EQ trait of Self Awareness, this cultural adjustment period could be brief, but rough. For us all.

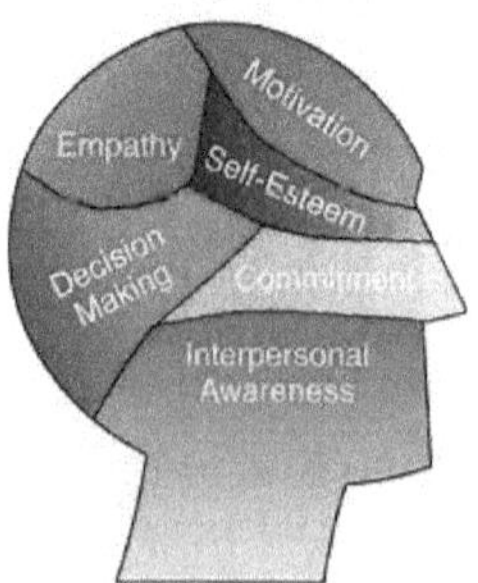

As mentioned in the opening, I've been through almost every conceivable dating scenario from "The Friend Zone" to "The Cheating Triangle" to "The Big Wedding Reception."

This is an opportunity for you to hear raw, no-condom, nothing-held-back stories and discussions from a guy who is willing to shoot it right at you.

I'm confident that not only will you appreciate the frankness but that you'll be better equipped to dive into future conversations that arise between the genders on these topics.

Buckle up.

CHAPTER 3: Social Cash & The Handbook

12 years old. Awkward. Silly. Riding my bike and playing video games were more important than anything. Then one fine summer day, a neighborhood 12-year-old girl had a crush on me. Her 14-year-old female friend walked up to me and informed me of "the crush." The 12-year-old girl bashfully peered from over the 14-year-old's shoulder – looking right at me. I hilariously didn't

understand what the hell anyone was talking about – much less what to say to the girl coyly looking at me. I simply rode my bike back home.

A few years later, at ages 13 and 14, my neighborhood peer group began having sex. So many kids were having it, that I lied about losing *my* virginity a year or so before I *actually* did – that peer pressure was so strong.

In my mid-teens, I had a high school girlfriend for two years which was about as normal as any American high school relationship ever. And yes, we were having sex.

But that relationship ended when I was 17, and by that time, my direct peer group's sex scene had gone from quite a few teens having occasional sex to all of them having sex constantly!

At this age, I received my copy of the Male-Centric-Planet, Double Standardized, Rules & Regulations Handbook, written in 1950. It stated:

- Play every sporting event *hard*. Like it's Game 7 or the Super Bowl.
- Emotions that display toughness are encouraged. All other emotions are soft.
- Have sex with as many girls as possible.

The better you are at adhering to these rules, the more peer group accolades you can receive as being masculine. And nothing, I mean *nothing* is worth more currency than having sex with as many girls as you can – the more *attractive/popular* ones (defined by male centric society) give you more currency, but still: High Numbers Matter.

So, I quickly surveyed my extended neighborhood and found local teenage girls that would either:

- Be trusted by their single moms to be left alone with me in some room or floor of the house (unlike my household, where my parents didn't go for that one bit).
- Be left home alone by their parents. Once I established a sexual relationship with some teenage girl, I could continuously just ride my bike right over her house, walk in, unzip myself and add to my totals. Easy. Hey, I'm getting the hang of this.

This is great. I got so much social credit for my sexual activity in three ways: 1- Other males were happy to know that their male friends are equally adept at acquiring conquests; 2- Peer-group girls admired a guy that *other girls desired* – not some lame or corny dude. In addition, 3- society largely looked the other way at my endeavors - unlike drug users, politicians, and computer hackers that our culture seems to judge all the time.

Before you know it, exchanging high numbers of sexual conquests for social currency is an excusable lifestyle. But as I got older and had jobs and a full plate of social and community activities, I needed one more functional aspect: convenience.

Ms. Convenience

Fast forward to life after college, with Corporate America employment and an overall hectic weekly schedule. I met Ms. Convenience on a social website. Our "first date" was me going over her apartment and being able to smash in a little *less* than two hours when I honestly didn't expect to be inside her *that* soon.

From that auspicious beginning, over the next year or so, she worked out wonderfully in my life. Efficiently is a better word.

It wasn't just that I never had to take her out on dates. It wasn't just that she didn't call or text me a lot. It wasn't just that she never brought up the topic of a "relationship." It wasn't just that she was extremely sexually available for me.

It's that she was *always smiling and amenable and open* to all of it!

Ms. Convenience worked close to where I lived. Meaning when I was working *near home* (huge sales territory, sometimes I was, sometimes I wasn't near home) I could meet her at my place during her lunch break for sex (usually head, no need to shower afterwards for either of us). She also lived close to one of my community-volunteer organization locations. As she worked from home by herself frequently, I could swing by and bang her brains out immediately before or after volunteering.

I never was in her presence without having sex of some type. I never had to take her out to dinner, drinks, or anything social (not that I mind, but it saves me time when I don't have to). I never stayed longer than chit-chat before or after sex. Never had to spend the night because she had kids, and I had places to be. We talked on the phone about a few things in her life, but not enough where it wasn't still "convenient."

Discussion point: Examining the cascading emotional events facilitated by our arrangement.

- Surface level: She was ultra-expedient to my busy life in a big bustling metropolitan area.
- Below that level, her continuous cheerfulness in-person allowed me to never have even a wisp of guilt.
- The first two points above allow her to physically fit into my *overall rotation* and to emotionally reaffirm that what I'm doing is valid.
- Deeper level: A fully, efficient rotation of women allows me to validate and verify my internal masculinity via garnering social currency. The more I receive all of that, the more I feel better – about myself. Just like a hammer from Home Depot, Ms. Convenience is a tool to accomplish a goal.

Over the course of time, I get better at managing my rotations. Diversified rotations are like a stock portfolio. Which means not only am I *adhering* to the rules and regulations of the Male Centric world in which I was cultivated – but I am *thriving*.

Thriving in the sense that Ms. Convenience is the perfect, most efficient situation possible for a man seeking a rotation to receive social credit. It doesn't get any more useful as an object in my toolbox than her.

But there are emotional consequences to me getting those social deposits. Too frequently, there are withdrawals from the woman's emotional account.

Overall dating confusion happens when:

- My motivation is for a fully functional rotation, and the emotional boost and social currency that comes from it.
- I'll be frustrated without it.
- Meanwhile: The woman's self-awareness isn't established enough to know she'll develop romantic feelings and she's confused as to her *true* role in my life.

Predictably, what ensued was tragic. Ms. Convenience developed feelings of love that she held onto - even years *after* our last sexual encounter. She was shocked and crushed when I announced I was getting married even when we hadn't seen each other in half a decade.

- Her takeaway: "*Why not me*?"

- My takeaway: Empathically sad. Yet also completely baffled that she thought we were ever headed towards a relationship. I realized later she never knew about The Royal Penthouse Girlfriend Suite.

Supplemental story on social currency:
The Handbook states that "degree of difficulty" matters as well. A friend of mine while in his late 20s was living with his 38-year-old girlfriend. When she went to work, he had a continuous sexual relationship with her 19-year-old daughter. Whether or not you think that sounds wonderful or awful or worthy of a daytime talk show – the insanely high amount of social credit he got during and long after that situation was legendary!
It was like a Social Powerball Lottery payout.

Two Questions:

- *Would any of our efforts still be worth it if we could not get social credit?*
- *Would it still be worth it if no other person knew about it at all?*

Those are tough questions.

Let's see, when I flip through this Double Standards Handbook, I see that I'm allowed to get social credit whether I go into full details about each conquest or not. It says right here, look: "Even the *vague notion* that I have women sexually available to me stashed in convenient locations around town or around the country is enough for me to get social currency cash deposited into my account."

That seems straightforward.

To be clear, details usually do get discussed. Details as to how a particular conquest was acquired, or the degree of difficulty all get hashed out between peer group males. The more details, the more I can guarantee receiving social funds being deposited in my account. And it doesn't just have to be guys that hear these sex encounter stories. As we mentioned before, women frequently gravitate towards chick-magnets – guys who other women find desirable as well. And when women hear our sex stories, they "condone" our behavior, and bingo – more deposits.

The message is evident: My overall masculinity gets validated when society forgives me "sowing my wild oats." When multiple women have made themselves sexually available to me, I am "The Man." That's going back into the centuries of male-centric cultures. And in a competitive society, where every pickup basketball game is played like Game 7 of the NBA Finals, when I'm "The Man" and you're not?

I'm a better man than you are. Hell, I'm a better person than you are. Sorry dude.

I need to stand out in my tribe so that I can be recognized as The Alpha Male and ensure my genes are passed into future generations. We'll get more into biology soon, I promise.

So, to go back and answer the "*tough questions*" in the previous page: Mostly *no*. It's *not* worth it if nobody even remotely knows about my escapades. How else do I get social cash in my account? How else am I showcasing my masculinity? How else does anyone even know I'm upholding the standards set by a male centric society? If we don't tell anyone, it's like the proverbial tree falling in a forest when no one is around. Does it even make a sound?

And wait. Since this is all part of a greater discussion on "How we got here"; Why was this handbook written in 1950?

Chapter 4: 1950

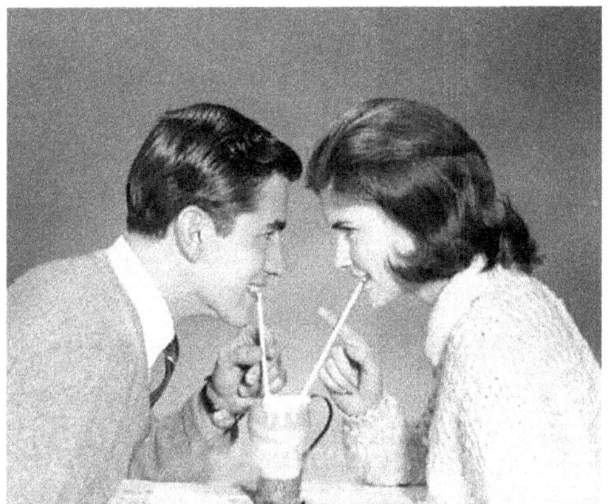

It's been a male-dominated planet for most of our existence. It doesn't matter one bit what the reasons could potentially be. It doesn't matter if men are physically stronger, or men are more competitive, or men have different reproductive biology. The list goes on. It's simply a fact that this has been a male-centric planet.

For our purposes, our male-centric history leads to current frustrations and confusions in our dating world.

In these United States, we can romanticize about the last "great" cultural era of a fully male dominated society: The 1950s. The previous centuries leading up to the 50s developed the mindset of: double-standards, objectifications, and sexual labels.

Dating interactions in 1950. There are still some elements we would recognize, some things we wouldn't.

Here's the 1950 script versus:
When I recently (yes recently, it doesn't matter when you read this) asked a woman out.

1950: Man asks a woman out on a date. Never ever the reverse. By 1950 customs, she is supposed to immediately give a yes or no answer. No ghosting allowed!
Man must meet the woman's parents so they can "look him over." And usually, the guy had to wear a suit or at least a tie.

I met a woman in a local bar. Bought her a couple of drinks while I waited on my friends to show up. Exchanged numbers and agreed we'd go out soon. Parents? No way, that isn't even considered until it's super serious. A suit? Nobody is wearing a suit on a first date unless we're *both* just coming straight from a corporate meeting.

1950: Man has the steady job, so he plans an elaborate date and he always paid the bill at the restaurant. After a few dates went by, couples declared their intentions to be exclusive by "going steady."
Although going steady meant that man is not supposed to date other women, societal

expectations of the time dictated that man can freely sow his "wild oats."

So, we've got cultural double standards established already. And it's just at the "going steady" phase.

I planned the date. We went impromptu and went to another bar just to continue hanging out. I asked her to pick up the tab in the second spot because our original restaurant bill was high, which she didn't know. Later she told me she had an issue with that, but we cleared it up later.

Woman is to remain a virgin until married. Furthermore, society condemned the woman who breaks this unwritten rule, while condoning men's behavior if they chose to pursue other women.

From that date, she and I became friends. I don't think today's man expects women to be virgins at all. But without question I'm allowed to be a stud and have casual sex without large portions of society frowning on me. Meanwhile, the same acts will label a woman a slut. Our male-centric planet has always looked the other way while we "sow our wild oats" and judge women for the same activity. Rarely does society judge men like me for "dating" women like Ms. Convenience or approaching women at cookouts because of their anatomy.

Overall, we'd like for you to have slept with *way less* men than the number of women we've had sex with.

The knowledge that your number of sexual partners is less than ours soothes our somewhat frail egos. To men, your low number reduces the fear that *you* might step outside the relationship sexually, which we can't handle whatsoever. That double standard is also still the same from 1950 – it's why we needed women then to be virgins.

However, even in neanderthal 1950, change was underway. As we mentioned, there were thousands of generations of male-dominated societies leading up to that era. But revolutionary ways of thinking about gender had started and of course, society had huge issues with it!

During the 1960s and 70s, there was *huge resistance* to hippies, free love and men growing their hair to the same length as women. Our culture was not happy about these changes:

Just like beach goers in Maryland.

All people were not alright about all those changes.

Change isn't a future event, it's an ongoing occurrence. Whether we're ready for it or not.

The emotional intelligence trait of self-awareness will not just change that the sexual dynamics of how men define their masculinity or how body parts are sexualized, but all the current gender "norms" from 1950. One day, it will all seem as antiquated as a typewriter.

CHAPTER 5: Mouth Wide Open

The sound that lasts in *my* mind is My Date's laughter. She was laughing so hard at her futile efforts to put Ms. Lesbian's right breast in her mouth. Not that she wasn't trying. She was opening her mouth as wide as she could. . . but… it was like trying to put your mouth around a soccer ball or a watermelon.

She was also laughing at me. Or rather, with me. I had my same struggles with the left breast. And seeing her make the same pitiful attempts cracked both of us up. It felt like I *could* get more than the nipple in my mouth. But directly observing how much of Ms. Lesbian's breast remained *uncovered* despite My Date's attempts to engulf it, made me realize the same was happening on my side with *my* efforts.

My Date's laughter also reminded me how happy she was in that moment. This is what she loved! She was a fully bi-sexual woman who was attracted to women and men. And that our date with Ms. Lesbian ended up in the back seat of my car was heaven for her.

We all had to drive in different directions at the end of our date at a bar in this strip mall (the strip mall looks like whatever you're picturing, trust me). So, before going our separate ways, we got into my car and pulled around behind the grocery store at the end of the strip mall and then all piled into the backseat. Then all three of us commenced to stuffing all the body parts we could into our mouths.

Despite the fun the backseat, My Date struggled with more than just trying to get her mouth around a huge breast. She struggled getting her mind around her own sexuality.

Rewind an hour. The real conversation topic for this chapter wasn't in my car. It was the three of us sitting at the bar talking during our date.

Two women who struggled to define and place human sexuality had one of the most open conversations I've ever heard. I barely said a word the whole time.

(At the time, my ears and my eyes were just as wide open as My Date's mouth later that evening.)

Ms. Lesbian was a romantic pursuer of female relationships. She dated and slept with women. She went to the LGBTQ rallies. The marches. Wore the rainbow colors. She had been open about her sexuality to the world since her teenage years. But of course, ran into backlash from her family and from society.

The ironic twist: She found herself still attracted to men. Just slightly. She didn't want romantic relationships with guys. She didn't want to have vaginal sex with men. But if some guy were cute enough, she wouldn't mind looking the other way from her proud Lesbian World and making out with the guy -- even *gasp* sucking his dick.

She did not enjoy the social-sexual conflict where she had to hide her closet heterosexuality within lesbian culture.

My Date, as she detailed at the bar, was never open to her friends or family about her sexual desires for girls as a teenager. She wasn't open to many people about it now. Her goal was to romantically pursue a man. Not just any man. She needed a man that could "handle" her desires to *have* other women – which of course she would share with the man.

I had been seeing My Date for about six or seven weeks before this date. And this was all our first time going out.

1950 and Sexual Labels

Before this date, I had considered myself open-minded to human sexuality. But I realized that my labels of straight, bi, and gay didn't fit either of these two ladies.

I thought, maybe now I should use a 0-100 spectrum of sexual preferences? 0 would be completely straight and 100 would be completely homosexual in terms of who someone pursues sexually and romantically? I thought Ms. Lesbian would be about an 80 or 85? Does this make sense? Because we could make this type of numbers system way more complicated to fit in more variables or we could make it instantly obsolete if it's too restricting. The point is that my mind had to change that day in that bar on human sexuality.

This is yet another item that our 1950s culture had no grasp of how to handle. Our society has had rigid labels. For a long time, we barely even acknowledged homosexuality. And just like Qatar with exposed elbows and knees, many parts of the world are still not "okay" with open sexuality.

Even when we, as a culture began using labels like "bi", it was still a nebulous description which left societal confusion on who you love, who you are, and who you are physically attracted towards.

We are the first generation to even to attempt to acknowledge that our square peg species does not fit into one heterosexual round hole. Future generations will negotiate a pronoun-less (he/she) genderless world. But for now, we'll struggle for bit.

For My Date, growing up in a school system and society that wanted her to fit into a box had her judging herself. Is she straight? Is she "Bi"? Shouldn't she know? Since the 1950s world isn't comfortable with her "indecisions," it places that uncomfortable feeling directly onto her.

Here you take it. We don't know what to label you, so you figure it out and get back to us while we finish writing up this lawsuit in Ocean City.

Right now, in our school system, it's a fine line between "promoting" homosexuality and making sure teens who feel they don't fit society's current static labels don't feel worse about themselves.

Most people in 1950 could not handle this discussion – and being able to even approach this topic – no matter how gingerly - is progress.

Small point. Inside of our current timeframe, our current culture has a double standard that works in favor of women. Since society is more lenient (not embracing it at all- just more willing to look the other way) when a woman dabbles in sexual acts with a woman, she is less likely to judge herself. Men are going against the planet's *huge* condemnation of homosexuality if they engage in the same act.

It's just the same as the declining moral of American Society as Ocean City's ban on naked breasts. The belief that *"Our whole way of life will crumble if we go down this path."* (which was also said about women getting the right to vote or allowing Black people to be in the same schools or sporting leagues or countless other reasons that "if this happens, then it's surely the end of all things." Chicken Little is not prophet.).

Again, in the future, this will be silly that our society struggled with sexual labels.

JUST AS A REMINDER.
IF YOU ARE OPPOSED TO
GAY MARRIAGE
YOU CAN SIMPLY
SAY NO
WHEN A GAY PERSON
PROPOSES
TO YOU

The emotional intelligence trait of self-awareness includes our grasp on our own sexuality. Our gender preferences, our intellectual and emotional needs, and our family background help even the rest of society to function more efficiently in this vast, wild world of relationships.

How 1950 mentality affects current dating

Discussion Point: The number of men still attempting to cement our masculinity, not fully understanding what drives us to pursue sexual conquests. It's on our minds, but not on a conscious level.

Also happening today: Some women are still struggling with sexualizing themselves on mainstream and now social media. Not fully understanding how they attempt to "validate their worth" in society by making themselves objects to gain attention.

Are all men and women struggling with these issues? Of course not. Is it enough that it affects the overall dating pool? Absolutely.

First Date. Value Assessment.

A first date. It doesn't matter how you met. Maybe at work or via mutual friends or on an app or a bar or a backyard cookout. Once you're physically going out on a first date, it's up to those two people to decide what happens *during* the date and if they want to go forward.

There are still so many varieties of things that end up in thought bubbles over our heads while we're on that first date. Good and Bad:

And while we're changing a lot from our 1950s mentality, men today are still far more likely to be thinking about sex *and sex only* in those thought bubbles over our heads. As we've seen, objectification and casual sex gives us much needed social currency. From the moment that first interaction happens, we're trying to gauge through the woman's level of attractiveness, just how *valuable* she can be to our social bank accounts. From that, we'll know how to proceed.

This exchange of female attractiveness leading to a high value being placed on her can be seen daily on social media. While millions of other topics and issues, serious and trivial, are shared and discussed on these mediums, select women have acquired millions of followers by doing not much more than displaying the attractiveness upon which society places value.

Do male models have millions of followers as well? Absolutely. But we subconsciously infer that in-shape men who display their attractive asset bodies are virile examples of disciplined diet and training and have worth to society beyond their looks.

Which leads to all of this being in play on any first date, without many of us being consciously aware of it.

"*How we got here*?" Here's another example.
In the previous book: *Too Simple to Believe*, we discussed how not all men are able achieve getting social currency equally. Meaning, depending on my social status, wealth, physical characteristics, and other attributes, I may or may not be able to "pull" women of a certain level of attractiveness.

The 1-10 "ranking system" detailed in chapter 3 of that book is indeed objectification at its ugliest. However, that system's current real-world application is that men are still seeking to m*aximize* what they can "pull" within the confines of their own limitations.

I strongly denounce that "system" for its past content. I strongly hope it will be in stark contrast to our future, more balanced society. But unfortunately, much of that system still has existing implications in our dating environment.

Case in point: An overweight male who doesn't have his own place or car and has little to no income may not be able to date the aforementioned social media model with millions of followers. Conversely the charming, in-shape, international real estate mogul may have a *selection* of social media models aboard his yacht. The shallowness of this social paradox doesn't minimize its ongoing reality.

Therefore, in those thought bubbles over our heads in early dating, men can be thinking about all of this, but not *saying* any of this because we're not consciously aware of it. This can lead to confusion and frustration for both people involved.

For men, the frustration stems from projecting that women wouldn't be able handle our desires for sex and sex only. So, we dance around the subject – leading to our own frustrations in which we commiserate with other guys: *"What's wrong with women*".

Let me clarify that frustration before we move on. While men are searching for a girlfriend or wife-material first, that girlfriend may not be you, but we still may want to sleep with you while searching for *her*. When you develop feelings, or don't give us the sexual efficiency we "need" within our overall lives, we get frustrated.

When we *don't* get a Ms. Convenience to work smoothly within our rotations, we throw mini-temper tantrums. "*What's up with these chicks catching feelings and wanting more of my time*" is the opening statement for about 10,000 phone and bar conversations I've had through the years with my male friends. It's the #1 complaint of all time. It's also just a great male-bonding conversation, right up there with the soliloquy: How I Personally Would Improve Our Local Favorite Sports Team.

How do we get around this? Seriously? Do we verbalize this in the Early Dating Phase? Do we state this clearly on a dating profile? I guess. But maybe this is something future generations will tackle better than we can now. What are your thoughts? I'm open for ideas. Let's get another round so we can talk about it a little more. Oh wait, this is a book. Never mind, keep reading.

Because I might be saying all the right things while we're hanging out for the first time. I uh, saw everything I needed to see to uh, confirm my decision when you walked to the restroom after the waiter brought us our drinks. And now I know what *my* objective is, well then, the real hard part is: *How do I tell you that*? Are you going to be ok with blunt honesty? How I even word that? How do I communicate, that at this level, I want social-sexual efficiency?

Here's how. Change is coming in the sense that within an overall society with High Emotional IQ (EQ) I won't need to accumulate as many sex episodes as possible to define or enhance my societal masculinity.

When I won't have to chase statistics to gain masculinity social points then the whole dating equation will be balanced. Similarly, self-awareness via women on what they expect and what they've experienced will lead to dating situations being more balanced. Less confusing.

Does this mean that men will one day just turn down all opportunities for "convenience and efficiency" on future first dates? Nope. It just means we won't feel as much subconscious pressure from society

For now, just like naked breasts in Ocean City, we're not ready for double standards and all that pressure to completely go away. Not yet.

Chapter 6: Erection versus Emotions

Why aren't we ready for it? Why are we pushing back? Why are we still okay with blatant gender un-balance and double standards? It's almost as if we're still holding on to the ideologies of our Neanderthal ancestors where The Alpha Male has the best chance to get his genes passed on to future generations.

No worries. Society is always slow to change. 100 years ago, we had to have a full movement to make sure women could cast a ballot in elections. Abolishing slavery, ending Jim Crow, and establishing voting rights all took time. In those moments, during those movements, much of society pushed back. It's part of our nature to resist change.

This movement is up against multiple previous generations – if not the entirety of humans on planet earth – used to defining our sexuality through our biology.

Lifetime Channel Flight Delay

From the last time I slept with Ms. Lifetime Channel until today, more than five years had passed. When we made the plans to reconnect and sleep together at her place, we were both excited *not just* for the impending sex, but to see each other after all those years.

Now I absolutely wanted to spend time talking to her and hearing how life had been. But somehow, we actually climbed into her bed within three minutes of me completing an hour drive and arriving at her house.

Even though I cognitively knew we were eventually going to have sex, I absolutely wasn't ready yet for seeing her body *barely* concealed by 1.5 ounces of lingerie. Right next to me!

I guess... I was thinking ...we were going to relax in the living room for a bit? Honestly, I don't know what I was thinking. But it was system overload for me to be in the physical bed with her that fast!

Her breasts were peaking at me through her super-thin garment like "*Come rescue us, we're trapped in these clothes, set us free.*" I was hesitant for a few seconds, then her breasts asked again politely and sweetly to be rescued …and so. . .

I rescued her breasts, stuffing myself with them like a starving man that hadn't had any food in days. Why were they so delicious? Was it some type of seasoning? Is this paprika?

Now, it still hasn't been 5 full minutes since I parked my car, but I've got a serious erection *and* her breasts in my mouth! All I've got on are gym shorts. I see that she has NOTHING on under that flimsy garment and now with her body 85% uncovered I start sliding my shorts off and climbing on top of her, ready to get it in!

And she puts on the brakes!! HARD!! Screeching tires. She says while blushing and smiling yet still firmly:

"Wait a minute, I need to warm up first, I haven't seen you in years and you're climbing on top of me already.
We have all night, let's watch some TV and talk."

I know those words made sense, but the pulsing blood in my dick had my brain foggy. What did she say? Something that sounded like… *don't have sex*?

It... didn't... make sense. I was stranded on the runway. I thought I was cleared for liftoff, ready to get to my destination – inside her!

Ladies, you wonder why so many men want to speed right past foreplay? It's because our erection is full, and we can't make it any fuller with *more* foreplay. When we're ready? We're ready! Now!

Don't get me wrong. I don't mind foreplay at all, I enjoy exploring and pleasing a woman slowly. It's just sometimes I get the urge to zoom right past it because, like most men, I can get hard so fast that I literally:

Can't. Think. Straight.

We're like a light switch on a wall. It's on or it's off.

So, our biology is talking to us like a software-based customer service voice: *"Insert reproductive device now."* (Did you hear a computerized voice when you read that? I know I did.) When we don't comply, it gives us directions again.

"Insert. Reproductive device. Now."

What has driven men since our Neanderthal times is that Need Sex Now mentality. It's powerful! And when you add *to* that biology and the societal impact of "conquering" a female to add social cash and validate our masculinity? Wow! We have had a voracious appetite going back through centuries.

For the record, I rolled back off that woman and begrudgingly started watching the Lifetime movie she had on, which was just starting.

Flight Delay. Stuck on the runway. My life is miserable. Feels like I have a personal cloud raining on just me on this bed.

I was pouting like a 6-year-old sitting in "timeout." Mumbling to myself under my breath about how I don't want to watch some stupid movie when damnit: *Titties are still glistening from my saliva one foot away ...and ...we're watching TV!*

A few minutes went by, I relaxed. And believe it or not I started getting into the movie a bit. Then another twenty minutes went by and I was *really* engrossed in this Lifetime movie! I was yelling at the movie after an hour, *"Why would he go down those dark stairs when the killer is down there?".*

Then the movie was over and uh, she was warmed up - to the idea of my presence in her bed.

Flight Zero-One-Niner this is the Control Tower, sorry for the delay, but you are cleared for takeoff.

Let's see, I got to her place around 8pm. It was 6:30am the next morning in the snap-of-a-finger and besides watching that Lifetime movie, we barely did anything else other than have sex. We hardly slept or took a break. Honestly, we didn't really "catch up." The end.

This episode is still about those very few minutes, even seconds it took for me to go from 0 to 60mph sexually (and then back to zero to watch a movie).

That's my biology fully at work. And it defines our sexual desires.

In that moment of full erection, men don't have any other thoughts on our minds whatsoever.

We're not thinking about what we have to do tomorrow for errands or work emails waiting on our reply. We're not *truly focused on the nature of our relationship with you.* Full erections completely take over the entire capacity of our brain. In that moment, we are sex zombies. Our whole evolution has led to this moment, a blood-filled dick and a willing female to insert it into.

We're definitely not thinking about emotional subconscious desires to get male social credit, even though the moments before and after our erections were driven by just that.

It's not going to be easy to alter our course as a society. We are used to thinking in this aspect as a way to keep our species going. Like all other organisms on planet earth, we all instinctively think about finding ways to:

1) stay alive via food/prey
2) reproduce.

Discussion Point: this basic biology has led us to thinking consciously about each sexual event, but subconsciously linking it to our inner emotions. Men and women have been seeing our psyches attached to the function of our genitals. And for good reason!! We are absolutely set up in almost opposite fashion!

A Flashback: Too Simple to Believe:

For the sake of easy, round numbers, let's say a female human can start getting pregnant at age ten and end at age forty-five. That gives us an uncomplicated number of thirty-five total years that she has available to conceive offspring.

Further, a woman is born with a set number of eggs that she will release one by one approximately every month. Big point: There are only a few days out of that month where that egg has a high probability of becoming fertilized. Once fertilization does occur, that takes that specific woman out of the reproductive-capable population for approximately one year (just for easy math).

Off the top of my head, I don't know any women with thirty-five kids, and there would definitely be a reality show about her if there was one. In any case, it sure as hell would take a huge toll on the woman, but the numbers speak for themselves: A healthy woman could have thirty-five births in her lifetime.

If you put this book down right now and pick it up at this exact sentence fourteen days from today, it's physically possible for me to have gotten thirty-five ovulating women pregnant in that amount of time, with ease. You're giving me more than nine hours to eat, sleep, and be ready for the next woman? No problem at all. That's how my biology is set up.

Not only is there no "huge toll" taken on me, but I'm enjoying this. A lot. I would venture to say that many of you guys who are reading this won't be able to finish reading this paragraph without taking a quick daydream to imagine how awesome that two-week stretch would be. Another group of guys are asking, "Nine hours in between women? How about a new woman every three to four hours?"

Let's bring it back for a second. Focus, gentlemen!

Again, we're talking about the female (take twins out of it for the sake of this example) producing just one egg at a time. As a healthy male, for the sake of my species, I make and store millions of sperm every single day. Out of the millions that I have stored on reserve, I ejaculate between 180 to 400 million of those sperm on each fantastic, toe-curling orgasm.

Post puberty, I can help to conceive offspring every single day of my healthy life. I *never* need to take a few days off out of the month for a *cycle*. I only get removed from the reproductive-capable population for a few minutes or hours. That's after I ejaculate, which of course, I love doing.

More then. I am physically equipped to do that every-nine-hour task. It's not just that I can get an erection in just seconds from mere visual and/or physical stimulation. It's not just that I can be *ready to reproduce* in the time it takes you to read this paragraph! It's that when I'm ready, it can be frustrating when men have to wait for the woman to "catch up" to our level of "ready." What do I mean?

That Ms. Lifetime episode falls right in line with our hypothetical situation outlined above.
Men are biologically equipped to be ready right now! We don't need to "warm up."

Let's get a final number to make this point clear. If you feed me a different, ovulating female every eight hours (instead of nine) I can max out at 1,095 annually. Not in a lifetime. Every year! (Of course, I don't have a job or much of a life besides sleeping, eating and sex but I'm not complaining.)

From an evolutionary standpoint, the greater number of inseminations a man achieves in his lifetime, the greater his chances are of being genetically represented in the future, and that is no small point ladies. Just because we *produce* and shoot millions of bullets, only very few *reach a ready target*, so for the sake of future generations I must be ready in seconds when an opportunity presents itself to reproduce. Literally. Seconds.

So, 35 children in a lifetime versus more than 1000 a single year! And that mentality driven from that disparity of why we're built differently biologically is what we're up against.

We've been using our biology as a backbone to our double standards. If you were feeling tipsy and excited from the "*uncover breasts, elbows and knees*" ideology from chapter 1, then sober up. This is a lot of tightly wound societal wires to unravel.

While I'm excited about our future, where female body parts aren't objects and men don't need more "bodies," I'm not sure we'll unravel all these societal wires in our lifetimes. Let's see if we can use EQ to sort things and get off to a better start in the early dating phase.

Section 2: Early and Online Dating

CHAPTER 7: The Parking Garage

Unraveling the wires in Early Dating

Unwinding those tightly wound wires will take time and effort. By all of us.

We can start by doing better in the early dating phase. That's the time frame during the very first few interactions with someone you're interested in seeing. If we get better at that phase, we can all avoid situations like:

Staring into a steering wheel in a parking garage

Early Sunday morning. Ms. Seven Dates woke up next to me in bed with only her panties on. Even though we did not actually have sex, I felt great about everything.

We spent the previous ending attending a house party hosted by one of her friends. We had a blast.

That party capped off six great dates over a little more than a month she and I had together.

So even though there wasn't literal sexual intercourse last night, there had been enough fooling around to reassure me that the *next* time we got together, there would be plenty of sex. Besides, she was about to be my girlfriend the way things were going. Who needs to *rush* sex when there's a full-fledged relationship about to happen?

We had been on dinner dates, lunch dates, hung out at a club with my friends and at a house party with her friends. Plenty of kissing and phone calls and texts before and after the dates.

We had met through a mutual friend. That friend was super excited that she had introduced us. And my friend's excitement got me in the mindset of: "relationship" from date #1. That mutual friend knew I wanted a girlfriend, despite me having a full rotation of women I was seeing at the time and felt this woman would be great for me.

So, headed into Date #7 at lunch downtown, I felt it was time to have the talk and make our plans to move into girlfriend-boyfriend status.

I was pumped!

Only a funny thing happened. While we were sitting at the restaurant table, I brought up the whole idea about us being "together." She uh. Well. She had quite the chuckle.

I still don't know her exact words because I was dizzy from the fog around my head. But I know she explained how it was silly for me to think we'd be on the verge of a relationship.

On that date #7, at that table, on the surface, I took the news well. I walked her back to her office building and then walked back towards my car in a nearby parking garage.

Took the stairs down to level P3. I climbed into my car. And then stared into the steering wheel for what seemed like three months, but probably was about twenty minutes.

It wasn't just the emotional ego crush that had me staring blankly into that steering wheel. Something bigger was bothering me. It was "Where did things get off track?"

How was I thinking this was headed for a relationship, and I was on the verge of a girlfriend when she was nowhere near that? Where was the disconnect?

We ended up becoming nothing. Not friends and certainly not lovers. Zero. And like most situations in the early dating phase, I never heard back as to why those 7 dates all went for naught. It's not like there's a dating review website where people leave posts like they're critiquing a restaurant.

Many people get frustrated over the early dating phases when they can't get on the same page with another person.

It's easy to move on when neither person is interested. That's easy, just keep it moving. It's also easy to know what to do when both people are excited and want to go forward with casual sex *or* a full-fledged relationship. Great!

But unfortunately, there is so much grey area. So many times, when one person is more interested than the other, it's a drain on everyone's time, money, and energy.

The Energy Drain was huge for me. Because it's not just the dates themselves. It's all the calls, texts and planning in between the dates.

Discussion Point on our own Self-Awareness: How can all of us get better at this? How do we figure out how another person is viewing "us" while still trying to figure out who that other person is? How do we speed up being in sync and getting on the same page?

How do we unravel the wires that have us so crossed up?

Let's put emotional intelligence to the test and see how that turns out.

1. It's not just that we need information during our dates. We need information without our own biases. We'll get that from not just asking the right questions but listening to that person's answer without projecting. What do I mean?

Emotional Projecting: What our preconceptions in life tell us about this person. The assumptions we make that aren't just about them, but about us.

In the situation above, during those six dates, I projected that *because* the mutual friend that introduced us knew I wanted a girlfriend, Ms. Seven Dates saw the situation the same way. How easy would me asking her that on date #1 have been? How much would that have changed my outlook going forward? I could have brought it up even in a casual way, just to set the table for future conversations about it.

I evaluated everything else *she* did on my own assumptions. "*Well, we're hanging out with her friends, this is obviously headed well.*"

More importantly, my experiences in life and my 1950s handbook told me that: Most women want relationships. Six dates are more than enough for us to be "going steady." It says so right in this handbook.

Even more: Most women want *me* for a relationship. I'm the one with the fully stocked rotation and any one of them would do backflips to get me to be their boyfriend. I'm the hot commodity here.

2. Self-awareness: Are we 100% sure that because this person has some advanced degree that they won't "accept" us because we didn't finish college or because we already have two kids that they won't want us for anything more than a casual sex partner? Are these realities or are we projecting our own internal emotional struggles onto them?

Self-awareness means *not having issues* over how you feel in your dress or your living situation or your current finances. Those are the things that you project into *their* minds on a date.

Let their answers be a guide to make sure you're *not* assuming you know them, or their story because of your pre-judgements. Pre-judgments about their house, their degree, their kids. Those can be just your projections about yourself.

I projected that because she was a professional woman, single, no kids and still at the age to have kids, that she wanted a guy like myself, with similar attributes. Silly me.

Early Dating

While the story about Ms. Seven Dates illustrates how assumptions can go wrong, it still has its own specific dynamics. Having a mutual friend put us together played a huge role for my outlook. But for most people, meeting as strangers has a different set of dynamics.

I wouldn't necessarily go too far down the rabbit hole of long-term expectations on a first date. First dates are all about just feeling someone out. (I left that last sentence wide-open to jokes, you know what the hell I meant.)

First date questions and conversations aren't about any right or wrong answers: They are about the energy/synergy, the actual attraction levels, and understanding how that person thinks.

There are so many parallels between job interviews and the dating scene. You're not just looking for the facts someone gives when they answer. You're also looking for HOW he or she answered the question.

High emotional IQ means being able to pinpoint what you were asking and crafting your answers to fit.

Discussion Point: The more we can ascertain from our dates in those early interactions, the more time we can save ourselves in the future. And that's what this is all about right? Efficiency. Not staring into a steering wheel in a parking garage trying to figure out what just happened.

Efficiency is even more important when you do not meet your date via mutual friends, work-environment, or social group. Meeting as complete strangers via online dating will require all your EQ antennae to be sharp.

Chapter 8: The Online Profile Dilemma

A female friend of mine was surfing through a dating app and came across a guy that made her pause. He was attractive enough for her to want to read his full self-description. In that write-up, he clearly stated that the only thing he wants from this site is future sexual encounters. While not being rude, he was being very blunt.

She didn't know whether to be offended or give him a standing ovation! The nerve to type for the whole world to read: *"All I want is sex*"?

Would you be offended? Or would you appreciate his honesty? You may or may not be interested in contacting this guy (she wasn't) but how do you feel about his statement? We'll come right back to this and get your answer.

Speaking of profiles and future sex partners. I did a ton of online dating. I've read thousands of profiles. I usually knew within 30 seconds of seeing a woman's full profile if she's available for sex and sex only and *not relationship material* for me. I can't do this with all women's profiles - not even close - it's only a small fraction of the profiles online that I can make that quick assessment. But for some, yeah 30 seconds.

How? And how so quickly? It may be *slightly* different for every guy but for me, it's not just her physical appearance that tells if she'll likely end up naked on my couch, but it's how she presents herself in her pictures and more importantly, her description of herself. Errors, typos, text-style shorthand, not a lot of depth, nothing creative. Calling herself "classy." All of those are high potential indicators for her being added to my rotation very soon. And we already know how emotionally important conquests are for a male's social cache. We don't even need to review the handbook.

Ok, we're back. Let's return to that guy who said all he wants from this site is sex. Did you choose being offended or having appreciation?

I did a quick survey of five female friends of mine by calling them up on the phone and asking them about the same scenario you just read.

"When you see this come across your screen, you think what?"

(And yes, calling five friends is the type of deep scientific, data-driven investigation that you'll only get in this book.)

Only one of them thought that *any* guy is an asshole for saying that on a dating profile. But that's only because she frequently sees many of the men being rude and crude with their language. She would want men with that outlook to type into their profiles:

"I'm not looking for anything serious."

versus:

"I just want to fuck/smash/hit."

All five female friends thought that men who write that into their profiles are doing women a favor. They appreciate the honesty and know to keep moving (or, if they're so inclined, to contact the guy).

A guy who is bold enough to type that onto his profile has a high connection probability with any woman who knows exactly what she's getting into.

What the women really liked was the lack of ambiguity.

Don't leave it open to me guessing what you want. I don't want to waste my time when all you're looking for is sex.

All that is great feedback. Honesty and all that. Sure. But then it leads to a huge dilemma for guys.

Most men want the potential for both.

That's both: I want the opportunity for a relationship, *and* I want to keep the door open for the opportunity for casual sex.

If I make my headline that - *all I want is sex* - then I just eliminated 90% of the women that might be a match for me for a romantic relationship. Because those women would go flying past my profile. Or if I contacted *them* first, once they come back and read my profile, I'd have a hard time explaining that I see them as a relationship even though my profile clearly states: "*All I want is sex.*"

Would I probably get some sex-only scenarios? Probably. Would they be women I want to be in a romantic relationship with? Probably not.

Huge dilemma. I need women for my rotational handbook 1950s guidelines, but I just can't exactly put on my profile:

"Seeking serious relationship unless you're not too bright or professional, but still somewhat attractive and meet my minimum attractive-level standards - in that case just seeking casual sex".

Did you get all that? Can I put that on a dating profile and get *any* hits whatsoever?

Because the reality is, sometimes I don't even know what direction things will go until I'm actually out on that first date. I could be thinking *"future relationship"* until she says something crazy, then I get a thought bubble over my head that reads:

And quickly, that thought bubble would lead to me changing up my conversation *from* more general "get to know you" questions *to* overt sexual flirtations.

Deep inhale... Slow exhale. Let me inject some EQ self-awareness. At that precise moment while sitting on a date, where I realize I am no longer investigating a potential relationship from this woman. Am I going to pursue her sexually now because I need another number on my hit list? More "bodies" on my count? Do I need to get this woman's clothes off just so I can have another story to shelve on my bookcase of sex stories?

In real time, that's what needs to go through my mind. Keep in mind, the more attractive she is, the more reward points I get added to my Masculinity Credit Card. Let me check my account status on my MCC app. It says I have enough points to get a free shot at the bar from my male friends in exchange for some good "*...then I banged her brains out...*" type of stories.

Being emotionally self-aware is realizing I can just walk away. Or at least be bold enough to clearly state my intentions. (I used to think I was Bold Enough but wait until chapter 10.)

Side note: Will there EVER be a day where a woman puts "I just want sex" as HER profile message ***without*** *being overwhelmed with messages from men in the same way women in the sub-set Muslim community in Qatar would be harassed by men for showing their elbows or knees?*
Just thinking out loud. Carry on.

Maybe that's the way to handle this going forward. Men can be overall seeking a relationship but can be Bold Enough to just walk away when it isn't going to be a future girlfriend. Or we can be Bold Enough upfront to say we're only seeking sex.

And while we're discussing boldness in an online profile, can we please state some ground rules?

Guys: Don't lie about your age or your height. Don't cover up your hairline with hats or wear shades in all of your profile pictures. Be bold. The woman that likes you will actually like you for you, not for who you're pretending to be. Plus, if you're "five foot four," and list your height as "five foot eight," she'll find out regardless as soon as you show up!

Ladies: Don't deceive us on your weight. No creative camera angle selfies or "shoulders and above" photos to hide that your midsection is not where you want it to be. At least one, very recent, head to toe picture should be a part of your profile repertoire.

Two of those would be better. (And no pictures of your cat or your plants please.)

And these asks aren't just because the other person is annoyed when you show up forty pounds heavier (ladies) or three inches shorter (guys) than what you stated or looked like in your profile.

But because your emotional stability is on display the minute you feel the need to be deceptive to get something you want. Being deceptive - *even in a slight way* - is communicating to the rest of us in this dating world that you're *not* comfortable with yourself.

If we choose to meet you and you *are* the person you presented yourself to be – great, that's a win for us.

But this book is about dating being a win for *you*. And if the *idea* of changing your height or your age to what it truly currently is - makes you feel uncomfortable - then take some time out. Step out of dating for a bit.

Whatever soul-searching you can do will help not just with your own confidence; it helps all of us to meet the real you.

Consciously, you're not deceiving us so that you can "get over" on us. You are subconsciously uncomfortable with your own height, weight, or age. Take some time and work on you. We'll be here waiting for you. The better you feel about you, the better the whole dating pool is for us all. Use that emotional intelligence trait of self-awareness to help all of us.

Chapter 9: 12 Years to Save

It's sad. Her husband was a "really good guy." Truly a loyal man. He's trustworthy. Dependable. Those aren't trivial qualities at all.

However, my friend's intellectual and empathic traits had received no air in which to breathe in her twelve-year marriage. Her frustrations about his lack of career ambition and personal interaction were always there, but after years of trying to explain her viewpoint, she had gotten nowhere.

Their communication on any topic of relevance was basically him lecturing her, with not just a limited vocabulary, but limited insights.

Add to the mix that the sex was never really that great, even in their early dating days. And it hadn't improved. And now, you've got one depressed woman.

She tried to tell herself that she should be happy. He's reliable. He takes care of his share of the finances without fail. He's always home. He's never running the streets. He's not a drinker and never touched drugs.

But even when he's home, he's not present. He's in the mancave playing video games and watching sports, rarely do they share a meal together, much less a stimulating conversation.

Those early dating conversations we've discussed aren't merely important to determine if you like the person or your intentions moving forward. Seven Dates to wind up staring into a steering wheel in a parking garage is nothing compared to being married to a person who can't communicate with you on your level.

Whatever level of discomfort you may feel in those first few dates when bringing up family background or dreams and desires is not nearly the discomfort you'll feel after a decade or so of dissatisfaction.

There's nothing worse than realizing that you saw the signs coming and ignored them. Hindsight being 20/20 vision isn't comforting when you're still in the relationship that you know must end.

So, using self-awareness, know what *you* need. And don't project that this person has those attributes until you find out they do through their own words and actions.

You need nurturing? Are they a nurturer or did they come from a nurturing family? You need someone with ambition? Listen to them talk about not just their current job but their future career.

If they've had problems with substances or have seen emotional trauma growing up? Are you ok with that? And have they shown the emotional intelligence trait of accountability towards their issues *outside of* their relationship with you? The more you know yourself, the more you'll see where any current date can potentially fit into your life.

We need to park this Twelve-Years-To-Save story right here to bring in a seemingly unrelated dating episode. Then we'll tie them both together.

Six Thirty or 7pm?

I just finished date number three with a woman who I viewed as one of the most attractive women I've ever gone out with in my life. In the phone call right after our Wednesday night third date, after telling me she had a good time, enjoyed the sexual flirtations and she got home safely, she invited me to spend the night in her bed that upcoming weekend.

Let me emphasize: She was a little out of my league in terms of her beauty and body. I uh, accepted her offer. That weekend arrived in what seemed like fifteen minutes after we got off the phone.

In a surreal moment right before leaving my place to drive to hers, I was quiet and wide-eyed. I was a little starstruck. I was silently stunned at what was about to happen. I turned off all the televisions in my condo and looked around my place like *it* was an actual person. I was communicating to my place:

> *"Wow I'm about to go have sex with this model-looking chick. I'll see you tomorrow condo*!"

Deep inhale… slow exhale… I left my place and drove 20 minutes to her development. I was supposed to be there at 7:00 pm. It was a little bit *after* 7:00 pm when I got a bit turned around driving inside her complex looking for her unit.

Finally found her place. Parked.

Knocked on the door.

Took another deep breath. I needed more oxygen, because to this point, I swear this woman has been *more* gorgeous *every* time I'd seen her. So, when she opens this door, will I be ready? I mean she might just have on a T-shirt only. Or less. She might open this door and I might pass out right here on this porch.

No answer.

Knocked on the door again. I realize that I didn't knock too loudly before because I'm still trying to compose myself. I'm getting ready for this visual.

Still no answer.

Looked for her car. It's not here.

Called her from the front porch. Not sure what's going on.

No answer on her phone either. Shit, do I have the right address? Yeah. I do.

Walked around to the side of the building a bit. Are the lights on in her place?

I called again. This time, she picks up.

And here we go.

She is screaming, crying, upset with a high-pitched shrill voice. I can barely make out what she's saying.

Something about...She's at her grandmother's house down the street...? Oh no! Is something wrong with her grandmother? I seriously can't understand what she's saying but this sounds bad.

She catches her breath a bit and explains.

Turns out, I was supposed to be there at 6:30pm. I'm a pretty timely person. Being on time is important to me. But this isn't about who got the arrival time right or wrong.

She explained that she was so upset about me being late that she began crying uncontrollably. She had called her grandmother who advised her to come down the street for a bit so she could calm down. She expressed that she couldn't believe that I would do her so wrong!

I was stunned. And still standing beside her building, unable to move. Her emotions were still very raw; she was trembling through the phone.

Moment of truth. Do I calm her down by profusely apologizing so that she'll come back to her house, and we can continue with our evening plans?

Or. Do I apologize lightly and push to reschedule for another day?

Or. Do I bite my lip, clench my teeth, and say: "*You're right, I was late,*" and take my ass home?

Because there was obviously a huge disparity between the size of her reaction and the level of my error. Even if I got it wrong that it was 6:30 pm and not 7:00 pm that we had agreed upon, that is not a reason to be crying so violently that you need a nearby family member to restore your emotional balance.

I chose option **C** and drove myself home.

Got back to my condo and it was shocked to see me.

"Dude! What happened? You're supposed to be banging one of the finest chicks we've ever seen right? Like right now! You were supposed to make plans to bring her over here next. I wanted to see her naked too! Dammit man. Talk to me! What happened?"

I know man. I know. Alright. Let me get into detective mode for a second.

I plopped down on the couch and checked my phone. It displayed that the first call I made from her porch was 7:21pm. Take away the few minutes of me standing there like a zombie, visualizing her answering the door, I probably was 15 minutes "late". Meaning *45* minutes late in her mind. And I see no missed calls or texts from her, checking to see where I was.

But that wasn't all. It wasn't just this episode of crying over 45 minutes. As I explained to my quiet yet baffled condo, she had shown signs before of being a bit emotionally unstable. I put my head back, looked at the ceiling and started to think back to our previous dates.

...that's right... she didn't want me to tip the waiter on our second date because despite his best efforts, the bar had run out of two menu items she had wanted. But it was super late, they were about to close, and he still was extremely pleasant and professional with us. Yet, she literally was looking at me signing the check to make sure I left the line for the tip blank.

... also... I remember now... first date... she relayed that story about some drama from a recent dating situation. Her story sounded fishy at the time – like everything didn't add up for her to be the *victim* she was portraying herself to be.

I grabbed the TV remote to find something to watch. Thought to myself: "Humans! Will show you exactly who they are."

Our best and worst attributes, traits and features are there on display for you – even when you're meeting our "representative" (that persona individuals show and create in order to hide character flaws).

Now this story: "6:30 pm vs 7:00 pm" is a bit of an *extreme* example, of course. But please do not underestimate *my extreme desire* to see her naked. I thought she was gorgeous. Not just pretty. Not just cute.

Which is why I had to compose myself in the first place before even driving to her house. And which is also why *not* advancing into a sexual relationship with her was tough! Plus, do you know the social cash I could get just for being seen with her? I wouldn't even have to tell anyone a sex story involving her. Just people seeing her and knowing that I'm banging her would do the trick. It may not be a Powerball Lottery Payout, but she would be worthy of a huge social deposit from my overall peer group – male and female.

I knew leaving her alone was the right thing to do. But it was painful for me - over the next few days - to not call or text her again for any future dates or visits. Because dammit, I was *this close* to seeing what she was going to be wearing when she opened that door. Don't tell me we're going to the buffet and then we drive there, and the buffet restaurant is closed! I know, they didn't meet food and safety guidelines and it's better off we didn't eat there. But I'm hungry now dammit! (Is this a sentiment only guys can understand? Do we need that Judge from Ocean City, Maryland to weigh in on this?)

The things that we want: sex, love and companionship, cannot be overruled by the moment. I get that. Balancing reason, logic and anticipation can be tough. But in our best moments, we can look past the moments in front of us and see what's coming down the road.

You already know what I saw down the road with her. If she's capable of being that distressed over 6:30 versus 7:00, then at *best*, I just saved myself from future arguments.

At *worst*, I just saved myself from slashed tires and condo windows being busted out – all from things I wouldn't be able to see coming because her level of *high* emotional stress is triggered by the tiniest of perceived infractions.

And in that Early Dating Phase, because we *hadn't* slept together, and weren't seeing each other yet: it was way too early for me to "call her out" on her behavior while I was still standing next to her place. She didn't owe me any explanation for her reaction. None. I didn't have the platform for that.

Besides, do you think that would be a productive conversation? Nope. Since she became so upset that *my first thought* was that her grandmother had suddenly passed, then calling her out for *that* over-reaction would just lead to an instant argument. Not to mention an additional emotional charge-up for me that I'd have to come down from throughout my now empty weekend.

But the EQ trait of self-regulation does more than just avoid arguments or dodge drama. With a clear emotional awareness of who you are, you save the other person as well, short-term, and long-term.

Knowing yourself upfront helps everyone.

Now let's go back to the twelve-year marriage. She did eventually leave him. And with their communication levels not being matched, he was crushed. More tragically, he was confused as to what happened. In his mind, he was being the same guy the whole time, he didn't change, why would she want to leave him now?

Because she couldn't view him fully in those early dating stages, she was unable to spare him from not being able to grasp what was happening now. He still loved her deeply!

All he could do was blame her in ways that didn't apply because in his confusion and hurt he couldn't comprehend why she would want to end a great relationship.

Knowing who you are and what you need in any type of relationship has a bigger impact on your dating efficiency than any question you ask your date from any thought bubble over your head.

Tracing back those last twelve years, she didn't realize *how much* she needed emotional resonance and intellectual stimulation in a relationship. In early dating, she couldn't connect that his family background was not full of ambitious people and that he wouldn't be either. Her family was full of academics and go-getters; she didn't know she would need that in a mate as well. Knowing yourself helps you know what you'll need from others.

Tying the two stories in this chapter together: Some guy is going to look past Ms. 6:30 or 7:00's emotional instability because he'll be fine with getting the social cash deposits that come along with dating her. She wasn't a horrible person. She was funny and smart. Some guy may already be on his way towards twelve years of being in a relationship with her and realize one day she is too emotionally taxing for him. And she won't understand why he's leaving her.

While I was still on my couch that evening flipping through channels trying to find something to watch I realized: I wasn't *just* upset I didn't sleep with her. I had been contemplating and mulling over a relationship with her.

And if the sex had been good that night and going forward? Man, *would I* have been able shut it down? Would I have been on my way to a 12-year relationship? What if I saw her histrionics *after* I had been sleeping with her? I'm glad I didn't have to answer my own question.

Sex and Long-Term Relationships

Since we're on the subject, let's dive further into sex as within the confines of a long-term relationship.

It's always debatable as to whether we need "great sex" in a long-term relationship. Of course, it's a plus, but in the true long-term, our physical bodies aren't going to function in the same way as we age. If you get married in your 20s, I *would* put more emphasis on sexual compatibility in a marriage. Marrying in your 30s or 40s? I would place a bit less emphasis.

(Not everybody is going be having wild and crazy sex past 50, 60 years old. And if you or someone you know is doing that past age 60? Awesome! Still, you can keep that to yourself.)

Whether we're talking about the 1950s or present day, dating someone who has no idea *who* they are or *what* they need in a relationship is a significant challenge. A lot of what we see as people "playing games" is simply just people simply not knowing what they want.

Even more of a challenge? Folks with negative views of themselves either from childhood or previous bad relationships or both. And at the very end of the spectrum, dating is tough when there are real-life stalkers, mirroring narcissists, and people who have temper tantrums if you're 30 minutes late.

Again, when you're sure of who you are, what you want out of any individual relationship, you not only help yourself, but you also potentially *save* someone else from future heartache. You raise the level of everyone in the dating pool.

Section 3: Casual Sex

Chapter 10: Destination: Casual Sex

Knowing yourself helps with first dates and early dates, sure. It can help save others down the road, wonderful. But it is absolutely a requirement before entering into the most treacherous, dangerous part of the dating world: Casual Sex Relationships.

Dangerous, why? Because when both people are single (The Cheating Triangle is Chapter 13) there are barely any rules! Contrast that with long term relationships like at the boyfriend-girlfriend level. Those have been following the same social dynamics forever. Marriage itself? That is literally upheld by state laws and religious doctrines. If people step outside the rules in those circumstances, at least they knew there were rules in the first place.

The world of Casual Sex Relationships? Unregulated. No set laws. Anything goes. Easily leads to confusion and frustrations. You think you're in one place with the person and then you find out you're not. There are too many issues and disappointments to list.

Let's be real: Casual Sex is a much more popular travel destination for dating vacationers. More people visit here than journey to Long-Term-Relationships-Ville or The Land of Marriage (otherwise we'd ALL have zero sexual partners *before* being married).

It hard to find a great committed relationship, but it can be even more difficult to find a steady, stable casual sex relationship that doesn't end in confusion or drama.

Easy to find, but the longer it goes, the more difficult it is to end amicably. One-night stands? Short-term hookups? They're not *as* harsh on our emotions.

The Casual Sex Relationship Destination is where I focused so much of my social brain power while trying to map it out. Most of the conversations I have had with female and male friends come from this topic. We're all trying to drive around and not get lost. Buckle up. Here we go.

Casual Sex Relationships Rules

Rule 1:

Know yourself. Know that if you need or want to be this person's eventual girlfriend or boyfriend, then state that. And then stick to that! Otherwise, the territory in-between early dates and serious relationships will not only frustrate you, but you will lead towards more frustration in the overall dating pool.

Example: You'll still frustrate this guy with *your desires for him* to be more than just a casual relationship. That's your desire, not his. I know he should see how great of a person you are, but that's "exhibit A" for putting your projections into someone else's head.

I know it's tempting to just roll with seeing someone in a casual sense because seeing/dating/sleeping-with someone you like is better sometimes than absolutely nothing. We all have social and sexual needs. And sometimes we just shrug our shoulders and say, he's cute. He makes me laugh. Why not?

But I have too many female friends, coworkers and relatives that come out on the other side of some on-again, off-again casual-relationship more damaged than when they went in.

Rule 2:

Continuously protect your emotions. Make sure you are just as clear as that guy on dating apps who says, *"I just want sex."* And just like those 5 women I surveyed that absolutely *prefer* to see that because now they know where they stand? Guys will respect that as well. Every male friend I've ever had has been in an early stage dating with a woman *we* weren't sure about but her instance on relationship or bust made him know exactly what he was going to do. Knowing yourself helps the person you're seeing as well as yourself. It helps all of us.

Hell, it helps your married friends who aren't even in the single world anymore from having to counsel you because you can't stick to what you want and keep going back to that same guy who clearly wants something different from you than you want from him!

But knowing yourself is only half the battle, right? Because it would help if the other person is clear on their intentions. Which as we're about to find out, isn't easy. I struggled a lot to communicate my intentions inside the wild world of Casual Sex Relationships.

First Plan: The Vague Territory

In those early dating stages, once I arrived at a Casual Sex destination, for years my plan was to just leave everything vague. What's vague? That means I just didn't say anything at all regarding a "relationship." I never brought it up.

I was projecting that women would pick up on my *lack* of relationship-talk and that they would take *that* as a sign that this was simply a casual sex situation.

I figured if they had sex with me and I wasn't pursuing them for a relationship or even discussing the topic, then we were "*all systems go!*" We're good right? Because I know that *if I were* after a relationship with an individual woman, that I would be discussing it, not shying away from it. So, I figured that any woman would pick up on this.

But dammit that was *my* projection. That was clear only in *my* mind. How in the human hell was the woman supposed to know that *when I am* serious about a relationship then I'll bring it up and make sure it's discussed?

Every human is different. All men don't have the same communication levels. For all she knows this is my way of starting a relationship. Especially when my *actions* say something different when we're in the casual dating stage.

My actions: I exhibit the following confusing actions when we're causally dating:

- I call you. Exactly when I say I'm going to call. And I listen to your life stories with feedback if you want it.
- I text back in a reasonable time if you text me first.
- Occasionally, we go out socially. Bars. Restaurants. Movies. Not all the time, but hey I happen to like going out and sometimes, I'm taking you with me.

- I don't directly say I'm seeing other women. I am, but I don't say I'm *not* either.
- I'll clean up my place from the last woman who just left (sometimes an hour before you came over. Which of course makes it look like you're the only one I'm seeing).

I figure you can't handle this truth:

I like hanging out with you here and there, but I mostly just want to sleep with you.

I'm guessing you're "ok" with this because I never said I wanted a relationship and we never talked about one. Right? We're good with this? I'm leaving things vague: Isn't that clear?

You know what happened with this? Shocker alert: Women kept catching feelings! And one day, this next woman confessed her feelings *so strongly* that it made me realize I had to change something in my early dating stages and leave The Vague Territory behind.

Guilt Snot Tequila

This wasn't regular sobbing. This was crying while coughing hard and throat clearing and sinuses full of snot. This wasn't that slowly, gently wiping your tears type crying. Snot was flowing.

Ms. Tequila, who I had been casually sleeping with for about 3 months (although relatively long-distance because she lived a 3.5-hour drive away) just bawled on my couch for most of a whole afternoon on a weekend we were scheduled to hang out in my city.

The plan was, we were supposed to get in a sober sex session first, then go out drinking all over town, come back and lose our minds with all night drunk sex. None of that happened. Snot Happened.

Stop laughing. What's the matter with you? I felt horrible! I don't *want* women to catch feelings and be upset or confused. I don't want the *guilt* of feeling, "What have I done?".

Now that her crying is slowing down a bit, I reflected that, up until this point in my life, I hadn't been able to figure out how to avoid arriving at this destination. This was the latest episode of feelings being caught when I thought we were clearly established as casual sex partners.

This was a huge moment. Because let's be honest, I wasn't going to *stop* having casual sex with young, cute, high-energy, small-waist-having, love-to-take-tequila-shots-and-party and then fuck-all-night women. Like her.

And I wasn't going to stop fixing dinner for some mature, sexy slim woman in my condo while neither of us are "allowed" to wear clothing for the evening. Meaning: Don't bring a change of clothes when we get snowed in for 48 hours. What you wear over, you can take those clothes off immediately upon arrival and put back on when you leave to drive home.

And I wasn't to stop driving over to that woman's house with tremendous hips and ass who always answered the door with 4-inch heels and dangling earrings and nothing else but a smile. I wasn't going to stop.

To be clear: I also wasn't going to stop my pursuit of a girlfriend via brand new first dates that I was continuously going on. A girlfriend will always surpass this rotation I just described.

But I must stop and try to figure out how to get better at this: Preventing this young lady and others from crying on my couch. It's not just the excessiveness of her crying. This is an overall pattern I've been in for a while, and like most stupid men, I keep getting caught off guard by it.

Of course, now as you're reading this, we all can clearly see how this kept happening. But at the time I was baffled. I had empathy for the women, but I also was trying to keep myself clear from the second-hand smoke of their emotional cigarettes: my guilt.

Talk to any group of guys, and this has been a balancing act since well before 1950. We want to "hit." But we don't want you to catch feelings.

Honestly, the guys who are ruthless enough *not to care* about your feelings whatsoever aren't doing all the things I end up doing. They're not taking you out. They're not calling you. They're not replying to your texts. And usually, they don't want to continue to have sex over and over. They hit. They're done.

I couldn't be like that. I don't want to hit it and quit it.

While I was wrestling with this in my head, I also ask of women: If you don't want to end up crying on some guy's couch, how much are you responsible for in monitoring the development of your feelings? Doesn't some percentage of this fall to women to not be caught up in a situation where their feelings aren't going to be matched?

If you're willing to:

- Come to my condo for sex at any time.
- Have me over your place for sex at any time.
- Not ask me about my whereabouts.
- Not ask me about my intentions or status.

Then I'm reading the signals that you're "ok" with the situation. You keep making yourself available. Then at some point – with crying or not – you state you have feelings. Dual Responsibility. Worth a re-visit.

Discussion point: Self-awareness is knowing what the stages of progressing towards a relationship look like to *you*. Of course, it's different for everyone.

But if you do not know what the stages look like, then you can interpret actions as simple as: "He texts me back" as "He likes me," without even realizing it.

My true projection to this point was that I assumed that all humans know what real relationship pursuit looks like. So, when I'm *not* doing all those things, I assume you recognize that and are "ok with" the current arrangement.

Everybody has had different experiences growing up, seeing relationships of the adults around them. We all need to know how *our* childhood affects our emotional intelligence in the sense of "*how the pursuit of love"* looks different than *"the pursuit of sex".*

If you know what the pursuit of love looks like, you'll recognize that within the actions and behaviors of the treatment you're receiving. Think of it as checking into a resort. Not all the rooms are the same.

Chapter 11: Your Hotel Suite Accommodations

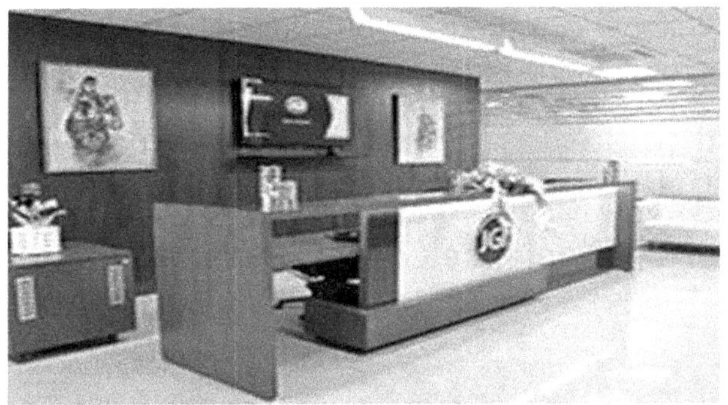

Welcome to your stay here at Christopher Dallas Hotels and Resorts. Could I have the name of your reservation?

Excellent then, thank you for that. One moment please while I pull up that information.

Ah, wonderful I see we have you in our Royal Penthouse Suite. That is the top of the line at our facilities. Please take your key card and proceed to the elevators down the hall to your left. You can follow our Bell Hop who is here to assist you with your baggage. Please enjoy your stay and we're here at the front desk 24/7 if there is anything you might need.

No matter what suite or room you get at any hotel, the marketing makes every single room or suite seem like fantastic accommodations. And if you didn't know any better, you can get comfortable inside of any one of them.

Read carefully as to what you're getting and not getting from each room.

Our Convenience Level Rotational Room

Also known as our 200 square foot booty-call room.

The accommodations are functional yet still exceptionally comfortable and you are welcome to book this room repeatedly. Calling and texting for purposes other than room reservations are available between the hours of 10am to 7pm, Monday through Friday. Alas, we are unable to provide snacks, room service or beverages.

Our rewards program includes two upgrades: One, to our basic cable television feature to play in the background of said activities. Two, window views of a parking lot instead of an alley.

Unfortunately, we are unable to provide overnight accommodations for this room. Most of our guests stay for the duration of our recreational activities only. Regrettably, this room does not come with access to our bar-scene life in the hotel lobby or professional meetings on our mezzanine floor.

Our Heavy Rotation Suite

Thank you for choosing Our Heavy Rotation Suite. Enjoy fantastic amenities in this 700-square foot room, like our free continental breakfast (after I bang you out overnight). Free Wi-Fi. Check in comes with our excellent buffalo wings or popcorn. All rooms come equipped with Smart HDTVs, and partial access to a refrigerator (if you leave food in there, I'm eating it).

Also, earn rewards including free nights out on the town and occasional social outings at our group events in the hotel bar. At all social outings, you'll be introduced to others by Your Name Only. Our shuttle service runs between 5:00 pm and 9:00 pm only, Thursday through Sunday (unless it's during football season, then service runs Tuesday through Friday).

Earn reward points by leaving out early after one final 6am bang out session. Final Checkout for this suite is promptly at 9am (We have things to do, including getting back to sleep or getting the room ready for another guest).

Our rooms are occasionally double booked with another customer; however, our staff (me) will work double-time to ensure your stay with us is recreational (I will still smash the Be-Jesus out of both of you, don't worry) and enjoyable.

Thank you again for booking Christopher Dallas Hotels and Resorts.

Again, if you don't know any better, you may think that Heavy Rotation Suite is great and that the treatment you get there is top of the line for our resorts. You may develop feelings after a few stays (despite the occasional "double booking," which we'll go over next chapter).

Other Heavy Rotation Suite features include: I'm not asking where *you* are. I'm not checking for where you're going or what you're doing or whether or not you called or texted me recently. I'm not asking you to date me exclusively. You're free to do as you please. In other words, read the fine print on this suite level: I'm not claiming you to be my girlfriend.

In my mind, this is so obvious that we're not going to be "together." Silly me.

The Royal Penthouse Suite

Our Royal Penthouse Girlfriend Suite

Luxurious accommodations await you as you bask in our 3,300 square foot Royal Penthouse Girlfriend Suite. Resplendent with panoramic city views and fine art from our 15th century French art collection. Located on our hotel's 50th floor, the suite comes with the emotional security that only full monogamy can provide.

Our security detail team (me) can accompany you even off the hotel grounds to your important social and professional functions. Even including: Your Friends' Baby Showers scheduled right when The Big Game is on.

Our staff (me) is on call 24 hours for your emotional, sexual, and social needs. Our shuttle system can pick you up from any location, 24 hours a day, 7 days a week, year-round. In addition, we can prepare for you any meal on demand from an array of culinary delights on our menu.

At our social hotel lobby bar scene and on our professional concourse on our mezzanine level, you'll be introduced clearly and audibly as My Lovely Girlfriend (First Name) as we are honored and humbled by your extended stay with us. We hope that you'll make these accommodations your permanent home.

Our rewards system includes ventures to all family and company outings – again with your full title as introduction.

Upgrades include our Fourth Finger Diamond Ring Program and Weekend Getaways to exotic locations.

If you've never been exposed to, introduced to, or heard about this level of service at The Royal Penthouse Suite from your upbringing or dating life to this point? Then my mid-level suites might still get you emotionally attached – much to my surprise!

Again, I'm thinking it's *so obvious* that you're not on the girlfriend track, because I'm *not showing* you the girlfriend suite level treatment. Silly me.

Chapter 12: Living Room PowerPoint Presentation

So now we have reviewed exactly what full pursuit of a relationship resembles. Personally, I had to still solve my own equation: How can I get women in The Rotational Suites to not catch feelings?

The Vague Territory is over. What's the new plan?

After empathically absorbing that crying and sobbing from Ms. Tequila, I was down for a few days. I knew I had to work on a new way of communicating. A new "*Casual Sex Relationship Format Without the Woman Catching Feelings Plan.*" And there is nothing about this in the 1950s handbook, so it's obvious men never cared about the women's feelings, just what women could do for us. I get it now.

So, I coordinated a full-scale meeting in the living room of my condo. Attendees included Mr. Couch, Mr. Futon from the second bedroom, and some other important furniture pieces. I was going to present to them my findings and the new direction we could take as an organization. I had prepared charts, graphs, and analyzed all the data we had compiled through the years. I put it all into PowerPoint slides and presented it all to my team.

"Ok guys, we've seen a lot of women come through here over the years, and unfortunately, all it does is end up in some form of misery. We're too empathic of an organization to continue down this path. We've got to be bold. Inventive. We need a new direction. I've got some information included in these handouts I'm distributing around the room that will help. Take one copy and pass the others around.

As you can see, the data shows that somewhere between dates one and three, the conversation pivots from minor flirtations to full-fledged discussions of potential sex. When we're sure we do not want a future relationship with this woman, but we still want to sleep with her. We absolutely must do a better job of stating up front that we're seeing and sleeping with other women.

Mr. Couch: *So, what do we do from here? What's going to be our plan?*

Thank you for asking that Mr. Couch. I've attached a declaration statement on the back of page six in your handout. You can flip to that now. I'll read the statement out loud.

"I appreciate your interest in having potential sex within our facility at the Condominium and Hotel Suites of Christopher Dallas. I want to state for the record that I am currently seeing other women. That being said: if you would like to continue pursuing seeing, dating, or having sex with me, it's highly likely that at some point, during the course of us seeing each other, that you'll meet one or more of these other women.

Factually stating, I am unbale to promise or assure that when you arrive at my condo for sexual encounters, you'll be the only woman there. I also cannot promise or assure you that when we go out for social activities, you'll be the only woman on the date with me.

Sincerely,

Management."

The meeting got a bit chaotic from there. The nightstand and couch were particularly upset.

Mr. Nightstand: *"I'm sorry, maybe I didn't understand you correctly. You mean we're going to tell women that there will be other women over from time to time? How in the hell is that supposed to work? Are you being serious?"*

"Absolutely dead serious. There will be no vagueness from here on out in our dealings within the world of casual sex relationships. I will not be cleaning up hair strands from the "last woman who

just left" from you Mr. Couch. Nor left-behind earrings, random bracelets off of you Mr. Barstool. In addition, Mr. Nightstand, any empty condom wrappers will stay in place - right on top of you - from the last sexual encounter. We're not hiding evidence from the previous woman, because the previous woman may still be physically here.

Gentlemen this new direction we take will be a bold one. It will take gumption. Guts. We'll tell any woman getting involved with us exactly what she's in for. We'll still reply to calls, texts and our normal casual dating protocols.

And again, that promise we'll make to future women will also declare that just because there will be another woman present in our facility that doesn't mean we have to be limited in what we do sexually.

Gentlemen, if we have two women over at the same time, we'll do 'em both. And we'll do them with a smile.

Now while we're in the middle of this meeting, I want to state our overall goal is to land a full-fledged girlfriend. If we think, even remotely, that any woman could be a potential for the girlfriend/wife suite treatment then this whole proposal never comes up to her.

*No need. If she and I get to that stage through vetting in our early dating phase discussions? Then, the rest of the women will be *poof* gone. When she arrives at the Girlfriend Suite status, all the other women will have vanished.*

Let's not forget guys. We can't continue this Single Life Path forever. Let me remind everyone here that Mr. Futon from the second bedroom has seen way more than his share of naked ass. He's getting creaky and squeaky from all these years of smashing these women. The data also shows that at this stage in life, he's supposed to be having our 6th grade daughter napping soundly on him, while I'm supposed to be checking our 3rd grader's homework on you Mr. Couch. All while The Wife is in her office getting her presentation ready for work the next day.

Obviously, none of that family life is currently happening inside this facility! I say we cut back on our amount of random vagina that comes through here by being bolder.

Gentlemen, this is bold. Daring. But I think it will work in saving women heartache, not to mention saving ourselves from extra work. I've done some research. Flip to page 14 in your hand-out and look at the data.

By my estimates, we'll have to "miss out" on approximately 66% of the women who would have normally gotten naked in our facility.

But folks, since we are a high-volume dating organization, the one-third of women who are on board with this will get the message. Meaning, finally no one will catch feelings because they have a clear understanding of what they're getting into upfront! Finally!

*I don't want to get emotional here guys, but this could lead us to *pause* guilt-free vagina.*

The meeting was calm. They saw the logic in my plan. Mr. Couch raised an arm for a question.

Mr. Couch: *What if it's only 20% of women that are ok with it? I mean, for the number of dates we go on, I'm going to end up with a drastic reduction in the amount of women's clothing that gets left on me overnight. I mean, most of the undressing happens right on me, right here in this living room. I don't know if I can take that level of reduction in action. I'm used to a heavy workload. This doesn't sound like I'll get as much activity as I would like. That's just me being honest.*

"Couch I understand and thank you for sharing. But let's look at the larger scope of what we're doing by going in this new direction. We absolutely want women to say NO to this offer.

The room was stunned.

"Not because that means they're virtuous or that this is some proof that they're worthy of "more" if they say no.

But because every woman who says no to this "deal" gives us more time back in the rest of our day, our week, our life. Mr. Couch, this means more weekend naps, more evening basketball games on TV with just peace and quiet. More time to reset our minds, not the whirlwind of our social life that leaves us drained so much.

This will truly be "efficient" dating.

Meeting adjourned.

So, I put it into action. The next time on a date, when the conversation escalated from flirtations to outright talks of *future sexual activity*, I put out my "statement" clearly. Boldly. And I found out. I so was wrong. Palm-to-forehead slap. I'm such a stupid, bird-brained, male.

What Exactly Went Wrong with That Plan

I had done my research. I had run the numbers. I "thought" it would be about a third of women that would be ok with the terms of this new deal. Nope. It was about 80% of the women that were fine with it.

I was as shocked as anyone when it was happening. In hindsight, I'm still shocked by it.

How in the world were 80% of the women ok with the following statement?

"On occasion, I'll be screwing some other woman that you don't know in my place while you're there."

How did women literally reply with?

"I'm not scared of you Chris."

Because my meager, male brain underestimated three things:

1. Honesty goes a long, long way. Just the fact that I'm capable of being *that* honest was huge to a lot of women. Give people known options and they may surprise you with their decisions. Women were used to having to figure out what a guy might be lying about (like his age or height on a dating profile). This level of honesty isn't just about other women being around. It's about knowing immediately this guy will tell you the truth even if it hurts your feelings.
2. Balls/Guts/Courage. Women were like: "Who is this guy? *He actually just said he was going to WHAT?*" We use the term "balls" for different expressions. In this sense women were like: "*The balls on this guy!!*" I wasn't going for that angle, but in hindsight, I see how it was taken that way.
3. Competition. As we mentioned in Chapter 2, frequently, women gravitate towards guys who are chick magnets. Women were more "ok" than I thought because when two women are sitting in my living room on Mr. Couch and Mr. Barstool, meeting for the first time (in the 30-45 minutes before I start with one of them) it gives them the opportunity that they normally would *never* have to size up the competition for Mr. Chick Magnet. And they were *not* backing down from that challenge. Her hair, earrings, how I respond to her, her whole vibe is fully on display and they are not scared of the fact that this other woman is also dating or sleeping with me.

To make this clear, this is not a threesome! I'm not asking any woman who isn't into women to lay one finger on the other. I'm not asking for all of us to be engaged at the same time. I'm not even saying I've got to "do both of them" in the same room.

In fact, I'm not even saying that I'm having sex with both. Or either one of them. Sometimes it was all just social. Make drinks, have food, and watch a pay-per-view fight. And yes, occasionally this applies to going on dates as well – two at a time.

These encounters were on a *spectrum* from being 100% social on one extreme to 100% sexual with one or both. It's two women in the same location – my condo or on a date. It's not a "threesome."

(Side note. Please let's not dive further into the conversation about what constitutes a threesome. I've been in threesomes where all of us did all things to all three and people invariably call it something else. The debate of what to name a "threesome" never ends and it's never agreed upon fully. It's a separate book and I'll be willing to tune into your podcast about it, if you have one. Just send me the link.)

But remember, my meager male brain conducted a full-scale meeting with a specific objective. That objective wasn't to have sex with two women in my place: *It was to avoid women catching feelings!* The objective was to be clearer and more communicative within The World of Casual Sex Relationships. I've been trying to solve this dilemma for decades!

My objective was to state up front that I'm seeing other women. I'm then backing up that statement by having women physically meet in my place or on a date *(at some point, not every day, not even close, people's schedules don't even match up that way, it's one out of 10 times you come over that this happens. The rest of the time it's the normal one-on-one*).

Did it work? Were there less women now catching feelings?

Well, mostly yes for a while.

But then it still all ended in disaster.

CHAPTER 13:
The Miseducation of Ms. Out of Town

For the most part, the new plan had been working. Until I had to re-evaluate my whole objective *again* after this one incident.

A sunshine filled weekend in May. A woman I had been seeing off and on for a few years who lived out of town wanted to stay with me for a couple of days. She was attending a weekend-long bridal shower in my city.

I stated how she was very welcome to stay with me; however, a woman who lived locally was also going to be at my place that Friday evening. I did what I promised myself I would always do.

I clearly stated to Ms. Out of Town that *while* she and I were going to do our normal thing (sex, in case you weren't thinking that it wasn't sex) Ms. Local Woman and I were going to be having sex as well.

Friday evening arrived. All three of us were chatting politely with drinks in my living room. Thirty to thirty-five minutes of chit-chat and small talk between two women who had never met ended when I abruptly began rolling Ms. Local Woman over on Mr. Couch, initially to receive oral sex.

I then rolled her over again and stood her up to remove her shorts to expose her fantastic backside to the warm living room air, bent her over gently and inserted myself into her from behind. What a view! Her ass is just: Magnificent.

A few feet away, Ms. Out of Town calmly sipped on her drink. Ms. Local Woman and I switched locations and went at it loudly, standing up in the kitchen, with her bent over in front of the sink. We were a few feet directly behind the still-seated Ms. Out of Town.

After a while in the kitchen, Ms. Local Woman, tired from her day and the sex she just had, announced that she was going to lay down in the back bedroom.

I took Ms. Out of Town by the hand, lifted her up from her seat. I pulled her dress up a little bit to slide down her panties. Then I pulled her dress down quite a bit to expose her splendidly spectacular breasts. She had taken off her bra when she first arrived. Her breasts truly deserve their own book written about them (objectification, I know, yes, I know).

I placed her down on Mr. Couch. I was about to climb on top when she insisted, I get a condom. I protested mildly, then I retrieved one from the master bedroom where Ms. Local was relaxing watching television.

Upon returning to the living room, I admired the sheer awesomeness of Ms. Out of Town's beautifully pigmented areolas as I rolled on the condom. I then lowered myself back down on top of her and inserted myself unhurriedly. We had no audience except the television for our own living room session.

Fast forward to 6am the next morning. I drove Ms. Local Woman to work (actually to the subway near my condo). I quickly drove back to my place and proceeded to have a great early morning talk (about a budding relationship she was excited about) then yet another sex session with Ms. Out of Town.

By the way, I get to tell this story because in the 1950s mentality that we still have today on double standards, I somehow get social credit. "You used to have 2 women over that didn't know each other and weren't Bi or Bi-curious and have sex with both? Wow."

Cash Deposits Recorded. Back to the story.

Ms. Out of Town and I finished our morning and went on with our weekend plans. I'm thinking *everything went according to plan*. I am being true to my word. I am being clear, not vague.

Fast forward to November of that same year. Ms. Local Woman and I had now been in Casual Sex

Relationship World for about three years. She and I were hanging out in a small random bar near her place. In this bar, she expressed her absolute deeper feelings for me.

She also expressed that another man was showing *serious* interest in her for a full-fledged relationship. Her pleading question: Was there any way she and I could work out into anything more, romantically?

Her overall point was: Even though this guy is currently pursuing her for a committed relationship, she is making it clear she would prefer she and I would be the ones to advance to that next level.

This wasn't exactly crying on the couch, but it was a clear violation of our original "contract." She wants to apply a little bit of pressure to see if there is potential for she and I to be together and move into Royal Girlfriend Suite status.

While her emotions were evident, and I felt them empathically, I still was thinking again:

Haven't I been clear that I am seeing other women?

Over the three-year time frame of her coming to my condo, Ms. Local Woman met a total of 5 other women I was dating. I would think she would be the *last* woman to think I wanted a relationship *with her* because in my mind (here we go again), I thought I was *being clear* that I'm not serious about a relationship with her.

In that bar conversation we were having, I absolutely was ok - even excited for her - with her getting into a relationship with this other guy she was mentioning.

So, that was it for us. We were done. But I couldn't help but take away that she *still* couldn't see what I was doing by having all those other women around through the years. I had a meeting with data points, charts, and handouts. This isn't still supposed to be happening!

Oh, it gets worse.

Several years go by. On a random Sunday morning I wake up to a text from Ms. Out of Town.

In this text, she stated she has loved me for years and wanted to have babies and grow old together and that she's grateful for our friendship, even though the love was unrequited.

I woke up in the morning, saw that text and picked up the phone and proceed to have one of the most eye-opening conversations in my entire life.

She had been drinking that previous Saturday night and a drunk mind speaks (or texts) what the sober voice will not say.

She remembered all the details from that night with Ms. Local and she admitted that even though I made it abundantly clear that I was going to have sex with her *and* Ms. Local Woman, she was still *SHOCKED* when I actually did it!

She couldn't believe I was having sex with this other woman right in front of her.

I was: Humbled. Crushed. Confused. Dumbstruck.

I asked Ms. Out of Town (our casual friendship now extends over 12 years) what message did she think

I was trying to convey by having sex with another woman I'm seeing, 4 feet away from her?

She didn't know. She is a highly intelligent woman and I have the utmost respect for our friendship (yes, every time we see each other we have sex, but that's not the point, she's an awesome friend). She could not surmise as to what I had thought was a *clear* message. Turns out, my "message" is still not clear!

Her overall feeling in those moments was that I must not care about her at all when I started fucking Ms. Local Woman on the couch in front of her. I stuttered and tried to grasp for words to ask the obvious guy question:

"But you didn't show that you were upset. I mean… you were calm, I was looking right at you. And then, you had sex with me 30 minutes after I had sex with her… and again in the morning. I'm SO sorry but had no idea you were upset. Or didn't want to do it. Or….?"

To which she replied:

"Well, I wasn't going to give up at that point and go home. I wasn't going to punk out. But yeah, I was shocked when you did it."

Deep inhale… slow exhale.

So, I didn't see it coming again. Both women in this overall story at a later point in time still expressed the same feelings that I had been thinking I was avoiding by being "bold."

In the moments after that phone call with Ms. Out of Town, all I could feel is that I'm an asshole. Again.

A selfish, manipulative Ass. Hole.

A whole ass.

I'm still repeating the same situations. I'm still projecting. I'm still assuming that my *actions* are clearly dictating the words that I do not say and have never said to any woman.

What I never express is this:

"I don't want a long-term relationship with you. Ever. Selfishly, I only want to have sex with you and be friends. Until I find a girlfriend/wife. Then we're done."

And what I end up *feeling* through my empathic nature is their rejection. I absorb it.

Through the years. Women have expressed:

"You like talking to me. Connecting with me. Sleeping with me. But you don't want to be with me and me alone. What am I missing?? What's wrong with me?

Why not me?"

That's heavy man. And unless you have NO empathy for your fellow humans, hearing that would affect you deeply.

Damn.

Put this book down. Come back to it. I need a minute.

Robot Love

OK. So, I tried to sort my way through my thoughts.

- Why am I doing this? Having sex with women I don't even want to consider for a girlfriend?
- Is it because I still want a girlfriend and my "rotation" adds up to one?
- Is it because I want the women to like me? Is it to validate my masculinity?
- Ah. It's because in a male-dominated 1950s world, I get credit for being a stud, and I need that credit. I need a full rotation (Like Ms. Convenience from Chapter 2).

I know that a big part of me just *enjoys* going out on the town on dates. I enjoy entertaining company at my condo, making some drinks, having some laughs. I enjoy the art of de-clothing a woman. But the consequences of the combination of all that outside of a committed relationship is: absorbing the rejection of each woman into each molecule of my body.

Self-awareness: It's difficult for me to be a robot. Even with Ms. Convenience from chapter 2, I still was involved with her life, giving her workout advice and being a listening ear for her family issues.

Robots in casual sex relationships can limit the interactions to just 3-5 minutes of chit chat before and after a sex session. Supposedly, that's what an ideal casual sex relationship should be. Not friends with benefits, but just: benefits. Just sex only. No mingling sex with details of your work or social life. I get it.

Unfortunately, I like to bond in other ways. I listen to your problems in other parts of your life, take you out (because I like going out). I might even motivate you in some aspect of your life where you might need it.

I just. Don't want to stop sleeping with you until I find a girlfriend, then I'll drop you and my whole rotation in a heartbeat.

And it's not just casual sex relationships. I bond with everybody. Coworkers. Family members. I can't help it. I like people.

But emotional connections get formed if I do more than robotic "benefits only" sex. So now I need another "new plan."

What will happen to all these Rotation Suites? I've been running this whole resort for years.

Chapter 14: Tear Up the Contract

The plan from here: Do not drive, fly, take the train or walk to any Casual Sex Destination which requires more than an overnight stay. No more Rotational Hotel Suite Packages.

The moment any dating situation veers off the relationship path, I need to cease all contact. It's the Royal Penthouse Girlfriend Suite or bust.

And that's no matter how much flirtation or sexual vibrations I get from her. Now that's bold. And it's emotionally self-aware to recognize my personal trait of empathy.

Far too frequently, bringing someone into the Casual-Dating-Main-Rotation Suite eventually *costs* me emotional currency that I can't afford. Upon checkout, anyone with an empathy credit card will see the bill due of unrequited feelings and experience sticker-shock.

Pushing the empathy to the beginning, to the front desk check-in, to that Early Dating stage is the goal. Being proactive to avoid that unrequited-feelings-bill, not reactive after weeks, months years banging out women in the Rotational Suites.

I'm tearing up the Contract that I created at the end of my last Living Room Meeting. It read as follows:

Casual Sex Relationship Binding Contract

- Thanks again for your reservations here at The Christopher Dallas Rotational Suites. Here are the documents detailing our casual sex relationship. Primarily, the location of our sexual encounters will be in my condo. Please put your initials here on this line.
- Part 2 of that document elaborates on how the potential exists for another woman to be at my place on any given night. Section 4 of part 2 details that you will receive at least six hours of warning before another woman arrives or will already be there. You can put your initials in this box next to Section 4. And another set of initials next to paragraph 7 of part 2 if you want me to wear a *condom* with either her *or* with you. I have to say most clients leave this box empty.
- A few other items: The stipulation that I'll communicate somewhat regularly and that you may indeed share your personal life issues if you so choose. Initial here.
- These two letters provide details on how I'll spark your intellectual side and/or bring out your fun side. Please initial both copies of the intellectual and the fun paperwork and sign and date my copy at the bottom. Please retain your copies.

- Ok we're almost done. This is the "*I don't really want you for the-long-term, however the time-frame of being in my rotation may last up to several months or years*" section. There are numerous pages and tons of fine print. Just read this over when you can and keep it for your own documentation.
- Ah, one last thing. We have an Ultimate Destination Clause of Rejection. As you can see the UDCR states clearly that *eventually* what you will get from all this is: Rejection. Sign full name here and we're all set.

Congratulations on being a brand new main rotation member. Are you ready to start having sex? We can actually start in a few minutes as soon as I file these documents.

Please go ahead and begin getting undressed. Leave your shoes and earrings on. Thank you. I'll be in you momentarily.

That contract will never be utilized again now. We can put it in the trash and light it on fire. It's not fair.

The Brand-New Plan

From here on out, when I'm on a date, when I see she's not Ms. Right *but she could be Ms. Right Now*? I have to resist the urge to want to stuff all of those tits in my mouth. I need to walk away. I've never really done it my whole life.

Ok alright, *possibly* there's an exception. I mean, all this is super easy to type when there's no in-person woman smiling and flirting with me. But, if the circumstances are *completely* lined up for it, if she's in a place in life where she doesn't want a relationship, maybe she had a very recent break-up. Then maybe there is an opportunity to venture into a casual sex relationship and draw up a contract. However, there needs to be another adjustment. The casual-sex *contract* can be revisited at any time.

Previously I would make women honor the contract they signed: "*Thou shalt not catch feelings for me, for I have stated at the onset that this is just casual.*" But feelings obviously change over the course of time, especially if I'm consistently doing those Main Rotation Suite Package services.

And I've got to stick to it. Why?

- Even when I'm not dating anyone at all, like the situation forthcoming with Lane 3 at the track, tragedy can ensue.
- Reversing the gender roles is just as unfair.
- The Friend Zone is awful.
- The overall process of dating is inefficient.

We have three more dating situations with three more discussion points to illustrate how leaving the dating world alone is best (for anything other than the pursuit of a girlfriend) then we're on to the Long-Term Relationship Section. Ready?

It's Lonely in Lane 3

Grad school. The university track is a great workout place. Some evenings I get the whole track to myself to get in a good sprinting session. 200 meters running all-out, 100 meters walking. It clears my mind as well as gets my heart pumping. But on that day in my usual Lane 3, I had a realization: I wasn't dating, sleeping with, or seeing anyone!

I wasn't just alone on this track. I was alone in any sense of a romantic or sexual life. I had to think: Do I know anyone who has a crush on me that I'm not giving the time of day? No.

Do I know anyone who I find attractive and is available, but I haven't stepped up to the plate yet and let them know I'm interested? No.

Am I forgetting someone I used to sleep with or date that still might be around? Damn. No one.

Now I'm not even running or walking on the track. I'm in lane 3 standing still with my hands on my hips trying to figure out how I got to this point. In life.

This is a small college town and I'm usually super-busy with research, but still. It's college. I actually had to chuckle. How long have I been like this? Date-less? This is what it looks like to be 100% completely single! Oh, well.

That weekend I found myself chuckling again at my Lane Three Epiphany when a house party turned into… me playing wingman... which turned into… a new dating prospect.

The dilemma: She was not my physical type. At all.

We can talk all we want about the shallowness of 1950's Handbooks. We can foresee that objectification of female body parts and 1-10 ranking lists are soon to be things of the past. But when you're completely single and lonely, we all can reach a bit below our normal attractive "standards" to just have companionships. And maybe a little fooling around as well.

For a few months in this little college town, I had a drinking-buddy / phone-conversationalist / occasional-sex partner. The word "occasional" must be used because sometimes even after the beer-goggles kicked in, I still wasn't always able to (this sounds terrible, please forgive me) see her as attractive enough to complete the night by having sex with her. Sometimes at the end of our outings, I looked at her and well, I just went home.

(One day, the previous sentiment or anything like it won't be said. Just like Miss 6:30 p.m. to 7:00 p.m. was a little bit "above my range" that I can normally pull. This woman was a little bit lower than the range that I can normally pull. One day, these 1950s standards of the masculine handbook will be antiquated. That would be fair. That is not today.)

How did things end in this situation? At the end of the relationship? You already know. It ended with unrequited feelings and me being empathically sad about it. Although years later, we did resuscitate a decent friendship.

Discussion Point: Just because someone is sexually and/or socially available and even when you are dating no one else on the face of the earth, the bill still comes due. At some point, you'll have to disappoint the person you were settling for and they'll be hurt.

50s Role Reversal

Let's go back to 1950 to see how fair this all is if we reverse the roles. Mary has a good idea that Billy really likes her. She is also sure she doesn't like him *quite* the same, but she enjoys his company. She continues to let Billy take her out to the local diner and send her flowers.

Billy listens to all Mary's stories about her family and her friends. He stays on the phone with her as long as she wants whenever she calls.

She is still wrong when Billy becomes upset that she *still* doesn't like him as much as he likes her. In fact, he's liked her from the early dating phase and likes her even more after a few months have gone by.

Mary can't be this selfish. She needs to have left him alone up-front the minute she knows she doesn't like him in the same fashion. She cannot give him a "contract" to sign saying he can't get emotionally attached but can still take her out to the diner. *She cannot stash him in the friend zone*. It is cruel that she would leave him alone the instant *she* locates a boyfriend to go steady with.

Discussion Point: Mary's self-awareness should know why she would continuously need attention and affection from a guy she isn't fully interested in. Does she just like connecting with people? Is this a pattern in her life?

My actions have directly led to feeling after signing said binding contract. It's like, I was just teasing the women. Tear up the contract.

And I should know better. I've been stuck in The Friend Zone before. It's the worst!

Maybe a Limousine Will Do the Trick

The question was could I get the timing right to make it dramatic? We're going to walk out into my condo's parking lot with our change of clothes in our bags and *come close* to getting into my car. As soon as she reaches for the door handle, I'll say "You know what, I've got a better idea."

I had worked it out with the limo driver that he should be way down in the parking lot. But close enough that he could still see me when I gave the signal by raising my hand high in the air. He knew this was a surprise to her.

And it worked – the timing that is. A woman who had stashed me in The Friend Zone for several months was now about to experience The Royal Penthouse Suite treatment.

The Plan: We were going for cocktails first at an upscale sports bar. Then, we had great seats to the local NBA team playing in The Big Game – almost floor seats. Then we were going to change and go to a Holiday Bash thrown by a professional society of which I was a member. It was a semi-formal event in a remodeled mansion just outside the city.

A friend of a friend owned his own limousine company. Bam! We're going to all our destinations via a stretch limo.

I gave the signal. The limo pulled up. I said to her: *"Let's go in this instead!"* The driver hopped out and opened the door for us. She stood frozen, still at the passenger door of my car. She was as wide eyed and open-mouthed as *anyone* in Chapter 4 of this book. Finally, she moved towards the open door. And away we went!

The evening was perfect dah-ling. Home team even won the game. The Holiday Event was spectacular, and she looked radiant the whole night. (We even had to change clothes in some back room inside the Mansion, which I thought was sexy and hilarious at the same time.)

And then on the ride back home, it was time to shoot my shot. I told her I did all this because I really, deeply like her and that I don't want us to just be friends.

She tried to sleep with me. I don't mean have sex; I mean physically sleep in the same bed with me that night. But it was awkward for her. I felt it too. As much as I wanted to make moves on this woman that I had liked for so long, she still saw me as a friend.

She had only agreed on the evening, thinking we were going to the game and a holiday party. She didn't know I'd get such good seats, nor did she know it was a mansion and she definitely didn't know about me renting a limousine. Because well, we were going as friends. She knew I liked her because of how strongly I'd hit on her when we first met. But I hadn't been able to move things along for months.

In the end, I just stayed my butt right there in the front row of The Friend Zone Movie – starring her. Pass the popcorn.

Sigh.

What happened?

Well, for starters, I projected that me giving her a sample of the Royal Penthouse Suite treatment would sway her. It's the same damn projection women made with me *all the time* that if they went all out and:

- Gave me the best head ever or
- Rode the hell out of my dick all night or
- Continue being sexually "convenient" or
- Cooked up a scrumptious meal.

...then I'd realize **gasp** she must be "The One for Me."

Nope and more nope.

Personally, I gave it my best foot forward. That is as good as I can do. I don't have access to a Lear Jet or a Yacht in the Mediterranean. But it wouldn't matter anyway! I couldn't make someone like me *more* by doing more things.

Plus, My Ego directly advised me that:

"The rest of the women I go out with would do literal backflips to spend an evening with me going to

these events. Much less scoot around town in a limo."

So, that's my ego and my projections talking. How non-emotionally intelligent is that?

Either it's a mutual connection or it's not. And your projections of what you can "*do*" for someone to get them to like you, are just that: your projections.

Discussion Point: I'm sure it's happened somewhere on this planet, where a limo ride or More Good Head has resulted in the person you like changing the way they see you romantically, but that's just not realistic.

The danger of any form of casual dating: When we know the other person likes us more and we continue to keep them around for any purposes, we are inviting them to eventually "catch feelings" and we can't be caught off guard when they profess their emotions. Meaning, to be fair, even Ms. Limousine has some responsibility for parking me in The Friend Zone.

Dating can be Inefficient. Here's the Data.

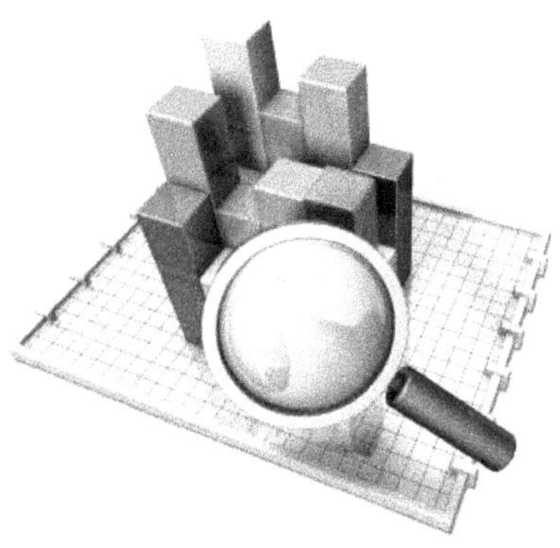

We're about to move beyond the dating sections in a bit. Let me be honest: Most of the time when I went on a new date, it didn't turn into anything whatsoever. Meaning, it's still a drag on time, energy, and resources. Being emotionally self-aware can help reduce the amount of time and energy spent.

I love data, so let's get into it:

On first or second dates: 30% of the time, in my dating experiences, neither party is interested in taking anything forward. Another 30% of the time, *one of us* is not interested enough to take it forward - and everything ends right then and there in both examples from this paragraph.

That's 60% of all early dates that end up going nowhere! Again, just my experience. And I was a volume dating machine for a decade.

The rest of my dates that did eventually move forward ended up in these four buckets:

- Platonic social friends
- Networking/professional associates
- Long-term or short-term casual sex

The final bucket is the smallest:

- Mutual girlfriend/boyfriend interest.

But overall, when I'm *constantly* trying to guard against women catching feelings, I'm not enjoying myself in this dating world. It's emotionally taxing to always be on my guard against emotional bill sticker shock.

Overall Dual Responsibility

Now, of course all grownups still have responsibility for their actions, once given honest choices. None of those women who ended up crying on my couch or texting me years later saying they have feelings would be in that emotional position if they had known and stated and up front what they wanted. I would have left them alone in the beginning if that were the case!

But it's tough to manage your feelings up front, right? You can't foresee how much you'll like someone three weeks or three months from now. You also can't see that they won't return that same interest even when you rent a Limousine while trying to impress them.

It's easy to look back see what went wrong, for all parties involved. In the moment, in those early dating phases or hell, when you realize *"that new coworker is cute,"* hormones are flowing, flirtations are happening, alcohol makes it even more enticing to move forward. But dammit that's what this book is for.

No, not to buzzkill the whole flirtation-mode, but to still have *some* part of you that investigates potential future outcomes. *Some* part of you can match potential outcomes with where you are in your emotional intelligence journey. From there you can add in *some* clarification comments with this new, cute coworker (still while flirting, don't ruin the mood please).

You can't let your projections and assumptions dictate that the other person you're smiling and flirting with is reading the exact same signals the exact same way as you are! Your emotional intelligence needs to pick up on how differently this person might be reading you and then *you* adjust accordingly. Conversely, your empathy can kick in when you know this person likes *you* more than you like them. We've all been on both sides of this.

Again: This does not mean you have to stop having those wonderful thoughts of a new potential casual sex partner. This does not mean you have to cease being excited with splendid thoughts of a new potential long-lasting romance. Just clarify with them what it is. You can do this!

And if you do decide to venture into the wild world of casual sex, keep in mind that The Contract can always be revisited and rewritten. Just add one stipulation which says this whole contract is null and void at any time.

That final contract stipulation has two results:

1: Men, like my previous self will throw a small temper-tantrum that we no longer have access to the sex (We'll be ok, you look out for *you*).

2: Men, like my current self, will be grateful that this didn't all end in rejection. Congrats. Grab the tequila. Here's two shots and a toast to you both.

And if it's for the splendid thoughts of a new potential romance? No need for contracts. This next section is for you. Long Term Relationships.

Congrats. Pop the champagne. Here's two flutes full of bubbly and a toast to you both.

The Royal Penthouse Suite

Section 4: Long Term Relationships

Chapter 15: The Emotional Bank Account

We discussed how self-awareness helps so much in Early Dating and in the World of Casual Sex Relationships. Knowing your own background and mindset helps even more to make emotional deposits inside of a committed relationship.

Conversely, being aware of our emotional background - how our life experiences make us the person that we are – helps us to be aware of exactly how we can enhance our partner's life.

The Emotional Bank account works just the same as any other bank account. The more money you have in your savings account, the better life can be. You don't have any issues paying monthly bills. You can order what you want at a nice restaurant. You can plan vacations to places you genuinely want to visit; not just places you can afford.

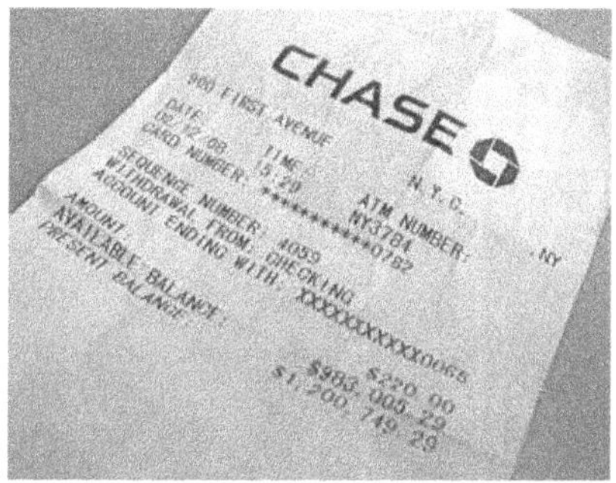

Having a lot of savings means you're doing a good job of managing your money day by day, month by month. And you'll be prepared when life throws a sudden emergency your way (and it will happen).

However, when your account has less money in it than what your monthly bills are, or the account is on zero or overdrawn, life is stressful. You may have to pay the electricity bill instead of another bill. Finding cheap food becomes more important. Nice trips are not in the budget. Stress level is much higher.

In a relationship, it works the same way. Emotional deposits directly into your partner create a healthy emotional account.

Daily Smiles towards your lover count. Planning a date night counts (not just the date night itself, but it matters when you plan it out).

Having a lot of emotional savings built up makes you more prepared when disagreements turn into arguments (and this will happen).

However, when you have made very few deposits in your partner's emotions, your relationship is stressful. More importantly, their viewpoint on *you* is stressful. Especially when you're "overdrawn" in their eyes. And "in their eyes" is an important phrase.

When you haven't been making consistent deposits into your partner's emotional bank account level, then even the rare, good deeds you do won't resonate with them in the way you might intend.

Your rare, good deeds, that you want to result in your partner's good mood get you closer to evening out your account - but you're still overdrawn - the account is still in the negative.

Consistent deposits based of your own self-awareness of how *you* fit into making them feel more loved is paramount. And consistent deposits will help their account to be full enough that when you need to make a withdrawal (you did something wrong) you'll still have enough left over in the account.

Leaving the bank account analogy for a bit. Your partner's subconscious not only recognizes what you do, it recognizes that you are someone who consistently places their emotional health as a priority, which makes them bonded to you with each additional deposit.

Without it being done consistently, their subconscious might be resentful or suspicious of why you're doing this *now*. Do you have something you're up to? Is there something you want from them in this moment? Are you making up for something you've done? Why are you being nice now? You're not consistently nice, this is odd.

The Cheating Triangle

Deposits in the emotional bank account of your boyfriend, girlfriend, husband, or wife helps with every aspect of the relationship. The one place I've consistently seen the *lack* of deposits show up is inside the cheating triangle.

In undergrad, I had the most Awesome Side-Chick (ASC) in North American History. Since I heard there are awards for this category, I am nominating her. And she will win!

At the time, I was simply happy to be getting sex that I *wasn't* getting from my girlfriend. Looking back on it all, much more was happening below the surface level sex.

My girlfriend and I were super popular around campus. And I liked that. I liked the social circles that we had with other couples. Behind closed doors? We went from simmering and sniping at each other to full out arguments.

But no matter how bad it got with any specific daily or weekly argument with my girlfriend, in the back of my mind was: "*See, that's why I'm going to go see ASC right after this so I can calm back down.*"

ASC told me early on in our side-relationship that she would *never* turn me down for sex. But it's not just what she said, it's how she said it. On the surface that statement is about sex. Deeper than that, it was that emotional bank deposit of: "*I'm here for you, I can support you when you need it.*" And she lived up to her statement.

If I had 5 minutes for a quickie before I had to run across campus for an afternoon class, she was down. If I had all night to have multiple sessions and then creep back to my dorm room at 7am, she was fully onboard. Since I had to call ahead to see if the coast was clear (either on her dorm floor or with her occasional roommate) she had time to make sure she never answered her door with any pants on – which by itself is an emotional bank deposit!

Give me a quick moment. I need to write her acceptance speech when she wins her Awesome Side Chick award.

Ok, I'm back. The emotional support from my side chick made my main relationship function better week by week. The arguments and lack of sex – lack of deposits – were tolerable because I was able to balance tranquility and sex from an external source.

This Triangle lasted a little more than a year. At that point, even with the support, I couldn't take the stress of the Main Girlfriend and left that relationship. Did I continue to see the Side Chick now that there was no Girlfriend to sneak behind? Yes. But it never developed into much more than sex and friendship.

Why didn't I just leave my girlfriend for the side chick in the first place? Never underestimate the shallowness of men: My girlfriend was slightly, but still noticeably better looking, and if I'm being honest, smarter. Plus, that whole popularity thing.

As we mentioned in previous chapters, the underlying desire for men to feel better about themselves through sexual conquests is strong. A big part of me having this side chick was that *she approached me* about applying to be my ASC. That is a huge ego boost! From the tiny number of my friends who knew about her, I received huge social currency deposits for the whole arrangement.

Break this down further, there is a woman who is acknowledging my very public committed relationship and still finds me so desirable that she is willing to sign up for being a complimentary piece of my life. She's willing to then contribute to sneaking around just to be able to sleep with me. Her actions - her emotional support of saying – *"I want you regardless of the circumstances"* is worthy of its own book. But.

There is also the other side of this coin: Even in college, with your fully adult personality yet to be developed, there is still a lack of self-awareness to her actions. Why be willing to settle or even belittle yourself for the attention of someone else's boyfriend?

- Is it about the guy (he's so great, I must have him)?
- Is about the girlfriend (she thinks she's so great and popular, I'll show her, I'll sleep with her boyfriend)?
- Or is it about herself? Is she worthy of having that guy - or any guy fully committed to her in a loving, supportive relationship? What did she see growing up from her family?
- Did she specially ever see her mother date a man that was someone else's husband or boyfriend? Was it ever normalized for her that "all men cheat" so she might as well sleep with someone else's boyfriend?

That's the emotional vibration behind her angle within the Cheating Triangle.

Let's also discuss the lack of emotional bank deposits by me that led me to being cheated on. By that very same girlfriend!

By always giving in frequently to what she wanted and putting up with her emotional outbursts in my efforts to "keep the peace," it created a "weak man" image of me deep in her subconscious. She lost respect for me and made it easier for her to step out on me. (I had it confirmed after the relationship ended.)

The irony of the Cheating Triangle: I was only "ok" listening to my girlfriend's rants because I knew I could be satiated by my ASC. But my being "ok" allowed my girlfriend to justify her cheating on *me*.

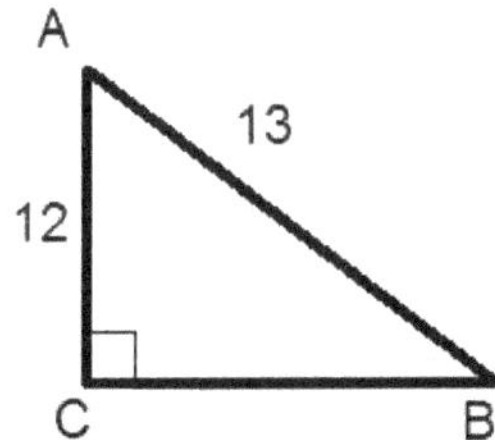

The third angle on the cheating triangle is when I'm the Side Dude.

Girl's trip to New Orleans. All her friends meet all my friends in a Bourbon Street bar. But the two of us end up talking and flirting way after everyone else leaves that bar. Thus, begins a torrid affair lasting more than a year.

Two huge takeaways for her emotional bank account.

1- Validation. She was questioning her own attractiveness and worth as a woman because she was getting so little attention and love from her husband. I provided: "*Yes you're still beautiful*" confirmation. Her mood had been down for so long that even her friends were happy she was finally seeing someone else because it lifted her spirits.
2- She was conflicted and really didn't want to be doing this. If her husband could've just stopped being selfish with his time, she would have never been in that situation. My takeaway at the time was that he didn't need to be married. He still enjoyed being out with

> his friends too much (and yes, still sleeping with other women as well). Self-awareness leads to self-regulation when we are able to know our own motivations. This woman's husband could have stopped her cheating at any moment by paying his partner more attention.

We all still have the mantra:

"If you're not happy, just leave the main relationship. Don't cheat.

That's still a good protocol, but it overlooks that we all *want* the main relationship to work! We invested in it in the beginning to make it a Main Relationship. Getting a new boyfriend or wife is exciting and emotional, and that excitement still lasts with us. It's not easy to just throw it out of the window – despite the flaws we see in it now.

Discussion Point: Entering a side relationship is all about the emotional deposits we wish were getting in our main relationship. It's not just about the sex.

But we all can prevent it from happening by using emotional intelligence to know ourselves first. Know how you can contribute the specific things your partner needs – that you can do without having to be prodded or asked or nagged about. Things that come naturally to you in the following three forms of deposits.

Making Deposits – Communication

So how do we keep that emotional bank account in the high levels of savings?

- Unique Communication
- Actions
- Passions

Communication. That word gets thrown around so much it has become a cliché. At this stage of the relationship, it's when us we use our excellent communication skills to increase the bond - not just to convey information.

Sure, it's great when your girlfriend can finish your sentences for you in a lighthearted way. That's an example of a communication deposit. But that's not what we mean.

It's *not* so great when you try to anticipate where your partner is going with a story or conversation and you assume incorrectly. That's an example of a communication withdrawal. But that's also not what we mean.

Huge communication deposits occur when you're frequently the only person who can feel and figure out what your spouse is saying when they can't find the right words – or when no one else can figure them out. When your wife comes to you because no one else really *gets* her – that's the huge type of deposit that bonds her with you beyond whatever the actual subject matter.

The Double Deposit happens when not only do you feel and figure out what your spouse is trying to communicate, but you then add to their joy *or* soothe their concerns.

Again:

- You feel their joy or pain.
- And then you add or soothe their emotion in a way that goes back to your self-awareness of your place in their life.

Lastly. There are times when even the most in-touch couple find themselves unable to covey important points. Take a step all the way back. Minimize all other distractions in the room (wait until the physical space you're in is quiet). Allow your girlfriend to speak what she is trying to say. Then you communicate back to her what she just said.

It's not just the words you're after. It's the way that she said it that you repeat back as well. Place emphasis on the things that you are hearing as important and then clarify those things by asking "Is there more?".

The formal exercise of repeating back the words and expression level of your partner is usually not an everyday or every week requirement. But it's when usual communication has still left a lack of understanding. However, when you're both able to finally break through after trying to get there? That is a huge emotional deposit. That person can trust that you'll go through the efforts to make sure that you understand what they're emoting.

And of course, what does the opposite look like? When your partner does indeed have the words to express their point, but you can't receive it.

Account Withdrawal.

It's okay to agree to disagree. If both parties felt their points got across. If you know you're dealing with a person who can articulate their feelings, it's your responsibility to make sure you hear and absorb complaints and compliments.

Not:

"Can't we just move on past all that."

Our desire to know exactly where the disconnects were so that we can square how we felt about our actions versus what we intended is big EQ. But you need to be empathic enough to want to know.

Without empathy, you won't want to hear how your actions affected someone else. At the end, people with low emotional IQ (usually with Victim Mentality) say:

"Well, you never told me what was wrong."

If you wanted to know. If you could receive it. You would know. Conversely, if you want to blame the communication gap on your spouse while declaring yourself the victim, there was nothing the spouse could say to communicate their concerns.

Remember: Emotional Intelligence is knowing when the other person isn't going to receive your communication. That's right back to Chapter 7 in this book.

Making Deposits – Actions

Doing things your spouse likes to make emotional deposits. Those are the things that are important to your wife therefore they are important to you. Her hobbies. Her Interests. Her relationships with her friends and family. The better you understand her connections to those things and why they're important to her – the higher the deposits are in your account with her.

Making Deposits – Passions

Your passions for your partner's interests and your emotional applause for their good deeds should be equal (or preferably greater) than your passion and energy for pointing out their weaknesses, shortcomings, or errors.

Your boyfriend is going to mess up! Your energy towards pointing out his errors, matters. Does it dwarf the energy you expend when he does something (at work for example) worth celebrating? Over the course of time, the golf-clap you do for his wins versus the hurricane force energy you display for his deficits can cause emotional bank withdrawals.

Again, if you haven't seen or experienced any of this in your childhood, it may be difficult to learn how to balance. You could be subconsciously sabotaging their hobbies and interests because you're not emotionally secure in yourself that your future spouse doesn't love those hobbies and interests more than *you*.

Your subconscious protects you. It builds up walls to make sure nothing can hurt you. The motivation to throw spears from behind those walls can by fueled by triggers from your own past, not your girlfriend. And it winds up showing in the ultimate relationship destination: Marriage.

Discussion Point: Ultimately, emotional bank deposits start with you knowing yourself. You'll know you're ready for marriage when you feel as though you are the best possible person to nurture, protect and ensure the emotional strength of your spouse. When you connect the emotional bridges between the strengths you provide and the needs your spouse has.

If you feel that no one else can do the job like you can of emotionally taking care of that person because no one else can "*see*" them like you can, then you're ready.

Chapter 16: You = Your Experiences

A former co-worker spoke to me specifically for this book about how she was sexually abused by her father. Her emotional vulnerability to elaborate on the adult implications has been crucial to her growth.

She does not sleep with any open doors in her bedroom. It's not just that doors must be closed, they must be locked. She has a favorite blanket she sleeps with every night for emotional comfort.

Through counseling and amazing self-awareness, she has cultivated a better relationship with her father and has healthy romantic relationships with men. It just takes her a while to warm up to a new guy because she needs to feel them out before she discusses any of this.

Key point: She also recognizes that her sexual wildness of her teens and early 20s years is due to her emotional self-detachment stemming from the abuse. That type of self-analysis is not superficial.

She has identified the cause, reconciled her past reactions and has forgiven her childhood self. Her current emotional vulnerabilities are worn on her arm, but under her protective sleeve. Standing ovation!

We've discussed extensively being self-aware and how that helps various dating and relationship scenarios. From our childhood through our adult life, we are all attempting through subconscious thoughts and conscious actions to balance-out our life experiences. We're trying to *"feel better about ourselves."*

What did you see, feel or experience growing up? Or what did you *not* see, feel or experience growing up? If you're not aware of it, haven't addressed *it*, you might reproduce or run from *it* in your relationships as an adult, whatever *it* is.

Emotional intelligence can help up us with Early Dates. And it can clarify some of the dangerous blind spots in Casual Dating. But it's an absolute must to have a great handle on your emotional background when it comes to any long-term relationship.

It's the goal of so many humans here on planet earth. Love. Commitment. A lifelong partner who is backing up your every step. Your loudest cheerleader. Someone with whom you can share your wildest dreams and your deepest fears.

What are factors that make a happy long-term relationship? Well, I wouldn't trivialize any of the common answers:

- Fidelity.
- Mutual admiration and attraction.
- A healthy sex life.
- A financial plan.
- Work-life balance.
- A shared spiritual connection to a higher power.

All of those are excellent building blocks. Are you self-aware enough to know *why* you desire a long-term relationship? Do you know your inner desires of what you can give, not what you can get? If you weren't seeking it and it comes your way, did you want it? Deep down, your subconscious may not see itself worthy of being loved and look to sabotage the whole thing.

A happy relationship starts with a happy you! All of us get our references for how to respond emotionally to life by what we saw and felt as kids. Not, prom queen or adolescence. I mean ages 0 to 7.

We're not simply learning how to talk, dress ourselves, and play with others, we're observing everything! We observe the patterns of behavior of those around us. Parents and siblings. And that becomes the basis of what we base our emotional decisions going forward.

So, it's not just:

> *"Boy, you sound just like your Dad when you talk about music. He used to go on and on about the exact same things."*

It's more like:

A mother that had 'victim mentality' in her interactions with loved ones. She would say incredibly mean things to her kids in one breath, even threaten them with physical knife violence and then flip and blame those same kids for how they mistreated her in the next breath.

Viola! That mother has completely created children who can't be blamed for anything, no matter how mean they are to others. That mother has created adults who will always play the *Starring Role of The Victim* in every scene within their romantic relationships. It's what they saw growing up.

None of us are even aware it's happening. As children, whatever we see growing up is simply normal life.

Unfortunately, millions of children who will eventually wind up in our overall dating pool have been molested, sheltered, micro-managed, abandoned or spoiled in their formative years. So many people are hurting because of it.

"Hurt people, hurt people."

That is a phrase much more about the deep pain many people have stemming from their childhood than it is a phrase about spreading nasty rumors at work.

On the same spectrum, millions of children grew up in nurturing households and enter the dating world incredibly idealistic. As we mentioned in The Redi Book: Triangle Games, it's incredibly difficult to negotiate the world of emotional manipulators when you never experienced it as a child. For those raised in emotionally nurturing environments, searching for perfection in a relationship can also be a lifelong struggle.

Meeting the Family

You and that special someone just crossed into the official boyfriend/girlfriend zone? Exciting! If you're not dancing at home by yourself in the kitchen in the days of a brand-new relationship? Then check your pulse and make sure you're still alive. New relationships are their own song!

So now, it's time to meet the family! It's still amazing that in 1950, this moment was frequently right before the first date. And the family was supposed to be checking *you* out (only if you're the guy, because you were taking their daughter out). Today of course, it's usually well-into an established relationship. Either way, in any era, this is a great opportunity to peer further into your spouse's emotional makeup by seeing his/her family dynamic. This is your opportunity to observe how your future spouse will subconsciously recreate this exact environment that you are in now. You are observing them as much as they are checking you out.

In my experience at this level, the dynamics of the nuclear family of your new boyfriend/girlfriend are a barometer of their childhood. And if they (your BF/GF) aren't self-aware, they will subconsciously sabotage all attempts to have a successful marriage, as their subconscious will attempt to recreate the drama of their childhood. This is exactly where my own marriage derailed. Unresolved childhood trauma. I completely underestimated it, even though I saw clear evidence of drama when meeting the family.

Conversely, if you're hosting a current boyfriend/girlfriend who is meeting your family for the first time and they do not warm up to the opportunity to engage, bond and blend with their potential future family? That is also a window into their soul and your future as their spouse.

This isn't lab research. I don't mean to make that initial meeting of family sound like you're staring into a microscope to examine contents in a petri dish. But this is your life we're talking about. And it's the closest bonded relationship we have as unrelated human beings. So, while there are social subtleties involved, this is not to be taken lightly. And you don't need to be the nervous one either.

Just like knowing yourself and where you are in your emotional intelligence journey helps in pre, or early-stage dating, just like reading the fine-line details in any casual sex contract, this is a place where your emotional knowledge of self meets its greatest task yet: Potential Marriage.

The Good News

Being emotionally aware is possible for most of it. It's a revolution that we're just starting. The distance we've travelled along our societal pathway since 1950 should be celebrated! There is more progress coming in our near future! The topic of naked breasts in Ocean City is about our collective growth.

Increased emotional intelligence through self-awareness will increase the emotional interactions of all the people in the dating pool. It will decrease the current frustrations and heartache for whatever romantic or sexual identities we desire.

We'll be able to drive, walk, take the train, or fly into new generations of efficient and fruitful relationship management.

Fortunately, so many people have *already* come to realizations about how their childhood affects them as adults. Men who recognized their mother literally never hugged them do the opposite and hug their kids without hesitation. Women who always wanted their father around at their sporting events show up at every single one of their kids' events. As long as we're consciously aware of our own baggage, we're less likely to overcompensate.

And as we mentioned, while we're discussing the journey of our own childhood experiences, it's also good practice to understand the background of our future spouse.

You wouldn't buy a house without inspecting the foundation. It doesn't matter how shiny the kitchen looks or how stacked the shelves are in the closets, if that foundation is shaky, you've got to protect your (emotional) assets versus this long-term investment.

CHAPTER 17:
The Bridges that Connect us.

Here's an equation we can use for our benefit: The closer the human relationship, whether as friends, co-workers, or family members, the more our childhood issues will come to the surface.

Why can't we see someone's deeper issues on a first date, or even a few months into a relationship? Because the subconscious can still be regulated at those stages by our conscious efforts to conceal it. The further down the relationship road you drive, the more the subconscious moves into the driver's seat.

It isn't just the amount of time that goes by. It's that the conscious will be able to keep the deeper issues in check as long as it's still actively trying to win you over – to secure a deeper relationship with you. Once that's achieved – and again, it's not on a set timeline, the subconscious can start to slowly inject more of its needs into this growing relationship.

It's the exact reason we *spend some time* in this boyfriend/girlfriend phase (and I don't mean to exclude anyone's sexuality here like my dear friend Ms. Lesbian, this goes for any identity, it's all the same phase). It allows us to see and experience more of the other person one-on-one before actually committing to them in marriage. And while the need to understand our compatibilities in terms of social, financial, and spirituality is great, comprehending and balancing our emotional backgrounds from our childhood to now is of mega-importance.

Currently, our emotional understanding of our significant romantic relationship partner could sound like:

- "He gets really mad when his team loses."
- "She needs her space first when she comes home from work to cool off."

Understanding the emotional space that your partner needs to occupy when they are stressed by some trigger is indeed important. Understanding that their anger directed towards their sports team losing is tied to the lack of affection given by their mother is bigger.

Why does marriage change things? How could a comfortable boyfriend-girlfriend relationship "change" when you cross into marriage? Because your mind knows this is the furthest commitment possible. We consciously and subconsciously know that this is as far as any relationship can go. The conscious mind might say: "I'll be myself regardless of the level of the relationship."

The subconscious can be thinking: "This is my opportunity to fully unleash my childhood issues because now this person has fully committed to me."

Depending on how deep its buried, the subconscious is protecting against any further damage to childhood trauma. Some people show their issues immediately. Example: Ms. 6:30/7pm. She let her issues out through her phone emphatically while I was still near her building. Her issues were on the surface.

Some folks begin to show their childhood trauma after a few months. Some during boyfriend and girlfriend phase or living together before marriage. For some, it takes going all the way to the alter, to the fullest commitment possible to unveil the full scope of deep-seated issues because this is the level where you're at your highest – your most vulnerable. At this level, the societal "what went wrong" questions can come our way if the marriage doesn't work out.

Too often, without EQ, we'll have to paint a picture that it was *them* that was the demise of the union. Our non-emotionally intelligent psyche won't be able to carry the weight of childhood drama and a failed marriage, that's too much of a burden to bear.

It's a commonly held belief that couples "do better" when they come from a similar background. I think it can help, sure. But if you're dealing with another emotionally aware person then it's more likely that person has already accounted for and is willing to discuss potential relationship derailments due to background differences.

Additionally, that same emotionally aware person can speak directly to the bridges that connect you – despite your surface-level background differences - because of their own emotional self-awareness.

But if we're being honest, we're not all emotionally aware savants just waiting to meet the next super high EQ individual. A lot of us could use some assistance being more emotionally aware.

Pre-marriage counseling.

"Hey, that was great and all about the bridges that connect and all that. I'm dating someone who is kind of unwilling to go there to understand their adult life actions regarding their childhood issues."

Great point. Let's address that in two ways:

#1 Do they regard it all as trivial and unnecessary to dig into their childhood?

Then unfortunately that's a red flag.

Refusal to touch the concepts of self-awareness can be detrimental to not just your relationship but to that person's overall life experiences.

#2 Are they merely unwilling to *fully* go there? Just saying, "Yeah, my childhood was rough, but I got it under control"? Examples:

- "My dad wasn't home a lot; he'd rather be down the street at the bar than home with me and my brother but it's cool, I don't need to talk about it."
- "My mom never told us she loved us and never hugged or showed physical affection to us, but I feel like it was normal."
- "My mom paid way more attention to my step-father and his kids than she did to us. Didn't matter to me. I'm good."

Any surface level dive into their childhood is a tougher situation to tackle – for you. You love this person, otherwise you wouldn't be in a relationship with them. But being emotionally vulnerable isn't something everyone can warm up to doing on the first attempt.

Use your own levels of empathy. The key is to direct the conversations towards that subconscious driver. Our subconscious is *going* to re-create or rebel against our childhood, in whatever direction that was, if we are not emotionally aware of it.

If your partner is not fully aware of how their childhood manifested their lives and they do not want to take steps to work on themselves: Another Red Flag. It's better to see it now than further down the road. I know it's tough to start over. I know.

If your own empathic conversations don't get you to the destination you'd like. It absolutely could be time to invest in counseling. Besides, if you are not a trained psychologist, you could alienate your spouse with trying to solve it amongst yourselves (again, the scenario is about when they acknowledge issues, but aren't emotionally aware of it affects the relationship).

Closings

How do we continue our societal journey away from our 1950s handbook? Simple to say, hard to do:

Emotionally intelligent parents create households and raise children who won't physically see and absorb their parents needing social currency deposits to boost antiquated definitions of masculinity or femininity.

Those children will grow into teenagers who won't struggle with gender identity or need social cash deposits of their own. Those teenagers become the young adults who won't objectify or sexualize women's breasts, elbows, or knees. Those young adults become grown-up future authors who will shun the creation or utilization of 1-10 ranking lists.

The balance will be there. And before you know it that 1950s handbook will be ancient history. A relic from our previous culture.

Picture this. A backyard cookout when a shirtless man or woman doesn't draw any additional *or less* attention than if they were fully clothed. Same for beaches in Maryland and communities in Qatar.

For the real-life people in this book: Ms. Convenience and I would have just become friends. She wouldn't invite me to her house on a first date and I wouldn't need to add another woman to my rotation. Or maybe I become Mr. Convenient for *her* in a truly gender balanced society. My relationship with ASC wouldn't be necessary for either of us. Her higher EQ wouldn't allow her to settle for someone else's boyfriend – she'll see herself as worthy of her own. Plus, my higher EQ wouldn't allow me stay in a relationship merely because of surface-level attractiveness or popularity.

Surface level ideologies also eliminate me being so enamored of Ms. 6:30/7pm. I'd still have gone out with her absolutely, but I wouldn't have been so crushed not to sleep with her.

Reflecting while in Lane 3 on a university track won't have me to reach for the next person that comes around to placate my loneliness.

EQ prevents both the twelve-year marriage of my friend and my own marriage from happening. We each would know our own emotional needs, see the family of our then-future spouses, and realize it's not a match. A higher EQ also prevents me from projecting "relationship" into Ms. Seven Dates simply because a mutual friend introduced us.

Yes, I will still have to sit patiently on the runway for Ms. Lifetime Channel to "warm up" despite my mind-erasing erection. But I'll try not to have a temper tantrum about it.

The Friend Zone situation still can happen, but there's a catch. I wouldn't have to hire a limousine service, because I'll realize that a woman will either like me, or she will not. I can't just ramp-up my treatment towards her and expect her to see *me* any differently.

Ms. Out of Town. Well, that whole scenario doesn't have to happen. I don't need to have a living-room meeting to manage my Rotational Suite occupancy levels. The Royal Penthouse Suite is the only accommodation available.

My Date and Ms. Lesbian won't have to hide their preferences or identities from heterosexual or homosexual communities. In fact, there won't be any need to use pseudonyms at all – for them or anyone.

How about a clear indicator on where we are as a society? The only individual we could openly discuss using their full identity was Judge James Bredar from Ocean City. Everyone else is still subject to some level of 1950s-style *judgement* from our current society and therefore needs protection from our antiquated communal mindset. It's embarrassing.

All these stories and situations will still be around as much as anything else in the past. They'll always serve as discussion points on how we can be more individually self-aware and collectively less judgmental.

From those stories to now, if one author can clearly see the progress in his own ideology then all is not lost.

More good news. The world we live in is already progressing. There are more people than ever embracing the ideologies of counseling, meditation, and self-examination of the emotional links between their childhood experiences and their adult behaviors.

Our goal at the REDI Network is that emotional intelligence can lead the discussions we all need to advance ourselves.

Including the discussion, we can start:

Right now.

www.ingramcontent.com/pod-product-compliance
Lightning Source LLC
Chambersburg PA
CBHW072056080426
42733CB00010B/2135

* 9 7 8 0 5 7 8 8 4 5 4 2 5 *